family

	POPULATION	AGE STRUCTURE (%)			POPULATION GROWTH RATE (%)	
		0-14	15-64	65+		(Ou
Australia	19,357,594	20.64	66.86	12.5	0.99	
Canada	31,592,805	18.95	68.28	12.77	0.99	
China	1,273,111,290	25	67.88	7.11	0.88	
France	59,551,227	18.68	65.19	16.13	0.37	
Germany	83,029,536	15.57	67.82	16.61	0.27	
India	1,029,991,145	33.12	62.2	4.68	1.55	
Japan	126,771,662	14.64	67.83	17.53	0.17	
Nigeria	126,635,626	43.71	53.47	2.82	2.61	
UK	59,647,790	18.89	65.41	15.7	0.23	
USA	278,058,881	21.12	66.27	12.61	0.9	

Central Intelligence Agency, *World Fact Book*, 2001

Births per 1,000 in population (in 2000)

Nigeria	40
USA	14
England	12
France	12
Canada	11
Austria	10
Japan	8

U.S. Census Bureau, International Data Base

In Norway, for instance, 49 percent of all the births in 1999 were to unwed parents. In Iceland, the figure was 62 percent. In Britain, it was 38 percent, and in France, 41 percent, in 1998, the last year figures were available. Even in Ireland, a deeply Catholic country where divorce became legal a mere seven years ago, about 31 percent of the births in 1999 took place outside of marriage, a figure on par with that in the United States.

Sarah Lyall, "For Europeans, Love, Yes; Marriage, Maybe," *The New York Times*, March 24, 2002

In 2000, 52 percent of women were currently married, down from 60 percent in 1970.

U.S. Census Bureau, press release, February 19, 2002

25.1 years—the median age at first marriage for women in 2000. This compares to 20.8 years in 1970. Women, on average, are 1.7 years younger than men the first time they marry.

U.S. Census Bureau, press release, February 19, 2002

1996, approximately 1,800 murders were attributed to intimates; nearly three out of four of these had a female victim.

U.S. Department of Justice, *Violence by Intimates: Analysis of Data on Crimes by Current or Former Spouses, Boyfriends and Girlfriends*, March 1998

In a national survey of more than 2,000 American families, approximately 50 percent of the men who frequently assaulted their wives also frequently abused their children.

Murray S. Straus and Richard J. Gelles, *Physical Violence in American Families*, 1990

53%—the percentage of men 85 and over who were married and living with their spouse in 2000. 12%—the percentage of women 85 and over who were married and living with their spouse in 2000.

U.S. Census Bureau, press release, June 1, 2001

H	INFANT MORTALITY (Out of 1,000)	LIFE EXPECTANCY (years)			TOTAL FERTILITY (per woman)
00)		POPULATION	MALE	FEMALE	
	4.97	79.87	77.02	82.87	1.77
	5.02	79.56	76.16	83.13	1.6
	28.08	71.62	69.81	73.59	1.82
	4.46	78.9	75.01	83.01	1.75
	4.71	77.61	74.47	80.92	1.38
	63.19	62.86	62.22	63.53	3.04
	3.88	80.8	77.62	84.15	1.41
	73.34	51.07	51.07	51.07	5.57
	5.54	77.82	75.13	80.66	1.73
	6.76	77.26	74.37	80.05	2.06

In 2000 12.2 percent of family households were maintained by women with no husband present, almost three times the number maintained by men with no wife present, 4.2 percent. 7.2 percent of the female family households had children under 18 years of age, and 2.1 percent of the male family households.

U.S. Census Bureau, *Households and Families Statistics*, 2000

In 2000 56 percent of men 18 to 24 years old lived at home with one or both of their parents, and 43 percent of women that age lived at home with at least one of their parents. In the 25 to 35 year-old age group, 12 percent of men and 5 percent of women still lived with at least one parent.

U.S. Census Bureau, *Living Arrangements of Adults*, 2000

601,209 total gay and lesbian families were reported by the 2000 U.S. Census. 304,148 gay male families and 297,061 lesbian families . . . . The 2000 numbers represent a 314 percent increase [over 1990 Census numbers].

David M. Smith and Gary J.Gates, Human Rights Campaign, *Gay and Lesbian Families in the United States*, a preliminary analysis of 2000 U.S. Census Data, August 22, 2001

In the 30 years from 1970 to 2000, the average size of the nation's households decreased from 3.14 to 2.62 persons.

U.S. Census Bureau, press release, June 29, 2001

Approximately 55 percent of all African American married-couple families had two earners in 1997, compared with 51 percent of comparable non-Hispanic white families.

U.S. Census Bureau, press release, February 24, 1999

Divorces as percentage of marriages [1996]:

UK	52
USA	46
Canada	43
France	41
Austria	35

Divorcemagazine.com, citing United Nations Human Development Report, 1999

Top 12 family vacation destinations:
Walt Disney World
Yosemite National Park
Yellowstone National Park
Washington DC
Disneyland
San Diego Zoo
Monterey Bay Aquarium
Sea World Orlando
Great Smokey Mountains
  National Park
Statue of Liberty
American Museum of
  Natural History
Acadia National Park

Voted by the readers of *Family Fun* Magazine

78 percent of pregnancies as a result of In Vitro Fertilization result in a live birth, of which about 50 percent are singletons, 24 percent are twins, and 5 percent are triplets.

American Society for Reproductive Medicine, © 2000-2001

3.9 million households were multi-generational in the U.S. in 2000; these are families where grandparents lived under the same roof with two or more generations of descendants. These households represented 4 percent of all households.

U.S. Census Bureau, press release, September 7, 2001

The amount of total contact parents have with their children has dropped 40 percent during the last 25 years. In 1965, the average parent had roughly 30 hours of contact with his or her children each week. Today, the average parent has just 17 hours of contact with children per week. A recent Roper poll showed that since 1976, the number of families that eat their evening meals together has dropped 10 percent.

Rocky Mountain Family Council, *Family Time Famine*

Of children ages 5 to 14, 1.6 million return from school to a home absent of adults.

U.S. Census Bureau, *Who's Minding the Kids?* Statistical Brief, April 1994

A poll sponsored by the National Parenting Association found that more than one-third of parents (36%) do not give any time to their kids' extracurricular activities.

Karen S. Peterson, *USA Today*, October 14, 1996

family

Cal Bedient
Mark Bennett
Alan Berliner
Sanford Biggers
Richard Billingham
Louise Bourgeois
Geneviève Cadieux
Sophie Calle
Chrissy Conant
John Corbin
Patricia Cronin
W.S. Di Piero
Laura Dunn
Nicole Eisenman
Margi Geerlinks
Travis Geery
Louise Glück
Nan Goldin
Linda Gregerson
Doug Hall
Robert Hass
Brenda Hillman
Marie Howe

Geof Huth
Ginger Krebs
Maria Marshall
Josiah McElheny
Robert Melee
Sean Mellyn
Olu Oguibe
Sharon Olds
Tatsumi Orimoto
Molly Peacock
Adrian Piper
Barbara Pollack
Ernesto Pujol
Christoph Raitmayr
Martha Rhodes
Faith Ringgold
Mira Schor
Sandra Scolnik
Jonathan Seliger
Tony Tasset
Chris Verene
Mark Wallinger
Allan Wexler
Jin-me Yoon

family

May 19 – September 4, 2002

Curated by
Jessica Hough, Richard Klein, Claudia Matzko,
Matthew McCaslin, and Harry Philbrick

Poetry selected by
Steven Henry Madoff

The Aldrich Museum of Contemporary Art

Museum funding provided, in part, by the Connecticut Commission on the Arts.
Erna D. Leir Gallery exhibitions supported by
Mr. and Mrs. John Bausman, in memory of Jane Bausman.

Education funding provided by:
The Barnes Foundation, Inc., FleetBoston Financial Foundation, The Albert
W. & Helen C. Meserve Memorial Fund, Nabisco Foundation, O'Grady Foundation,
and The Perrin Family Foundation

ISBN# 1-888332-19-0
© 2002 The Aldrich Museum of Contemporary Art
258 Main Street, Ridgefield, Connecticut, 06877

Editors: Amy Grabowski and Jessica Hough
Designers: J. Abbott Miller and Johnschen Kudos, Pentagram
Printer: Canfield & Tack, Inc.

Front cover: Sean Mellyn, *It's a Beautiful Day* (detail), 2000
Back cover: Jin-me Yoon, *Intersection V* (right panel of diptych), 2001

contents

I am the fourth of four sons, born in Providence, Rhode Island, in 1958 to Deborah and Charles Philbrick. Between the first and second son a daughter died at birth. Had she lived, I would probably not have been born. My father died in 1971 at the age of forty-eight. I was twelve. My mother died in 1980 at the age of fifty-three. I was twenty-one. I have been married for almost twenty years. My wife and I have a fifteen-year-old son, and a six-year-old daughter.

None of that is relevant to this exhibition; yet all of it is. Each artist, each poet, each curator, and each viewer and reader is colored by his or her family experience, and brings their experience with them to this exhibition. Because of this, we are all authorities on the subject of family. This exhibition speaks to an audience of experts on a subject that is universal. It is, as you might imagine, a diverse affair, with work by turns celebratory, personal, specific, loving, critical, sexual, resentful, playful, arch, knowing, and naïve.

The writing in this catalogue does not, therefore, attempt to present an authoritative portrait of the family today (we include a few brief statistical portraits), but rather gives voice through poetry to the intense emotions associated with the many roles in a family: mother, father, lover, partner, sister, brother, daughter, son, and grandparent.

The idea to use poetry to accomplish this was, no doubt, influenced by the fact that my father, Charles Philbrick, was a poet; he published four volumes of poetry and co-authored a textbook that was, for a time, the standard college text. He wrote this about the bed my wife and I now sleep in:

Plaque for a Brass Bed

Everything else is just furniture. This bed
Is frame on which, in light or dark, forgiveness
Weaves itself, and failure fails to matter.
Here love has worked, and pain has visited;
Here life has struck; here death may still the sheets:
This bed our garden, altar, engine-room,
The tablet of whatever testament our blood
Has written in our more than twenty years.

The very idea of mounting this exhibition was also, in its way, a product of my family: this time my wife Jane was the catalyst. She related to me a conversation she had had with Matthew McCaslin about the art world. Matthew felt that the adolescent behavior that some artists are encouraged to exhibit by collectors, curators, and critics was antithetical to his daily concerns, which most parents share, regarding housing, schooling, and money. The conversation piqued echoes of conversations that my colleague Richard Klein and I had over the last few years about the suburban experience (largely built on an idea of family), and intergenerational relationships between artists, their influences, and their progeny.

Working with our colleague Jessica Hough, we decided to ask Matthew to join us in curating an exhibition about how artists interpret their own family experiences, and the role of the family in our society. Matthew McCaslin is an enormously gifted artist who has exhibited widely across the country and Europe; his knowledge of the work of younger artists, and generosity in promoting their work, is exemplary. I was also keen to include Claudia Matzko, whose extraordinary art I have admired for many years. She also brings the breadth of her extensive exhibition history to the project, along with a rigorously analytical mind and a sophisticated eye. This is the second time in recent years The Aldrich has invited artists to work as part of our curatorial team, and it is a practice I heartily recommend to other institutions. Of course, the key is intelligent, generous artists, and dedicated, collegial collaborators; I am grateful to Jessica Hough and Richard Klein for embodying these characteristics.

The inclusion of contemporary poets in this exhibition catalogue furthers the commitment the Museum has demonstrated to poetry through the Aldrich Poetry Competition. I would like to express the gratitude of The Aldrich to Steven Henry Madoff for so deftly and successfully rising to the challenge of adding the rich and sonorous voice of poetry to this project.

Special thanks also to Amy Grabowski, whose dedication and profession-alism is deeply appreciated by all of us at the Museum. And to our able and extraordinary intern Laura Sawicki, I know I speak for all the curators in expressing gratitude for your hard work and good insights. Thanks also to Jane Calverley for her editing skills, and for assisting Amy in gathering statistical data. And our admiration to J. Abbott Miller, for suggesting statistics, and for bringing to this volume his great skill and clarity of design.

The assistance and advice of those galleries whose names you see listed in this catalogue is deeply appreciated. We are deeply indebted to those lenders who have so graciously parted with such wonderful works of art for the duration of the exhibition: The Bailey Collection, Pat Goizetti and Therese Quinn, Mr. and Mrs. Daniel M. Holtz, Dominique Levy, Frank and Nina Moore, Ivelin and Craig Robins, Ikkan Sanada, and George and Joyce Wein.

We are very grateful to The British Council not only for loaning Mark Wallinger's *Royal Ascot*, but also for their generous assistance in bringing it to these shores.

And, most of all, as always, our thanks to the artists whose works we are privileged to exhibit at The Aldrich. You are the family for whom this institution exists.

Harry Philbrick, *Director*

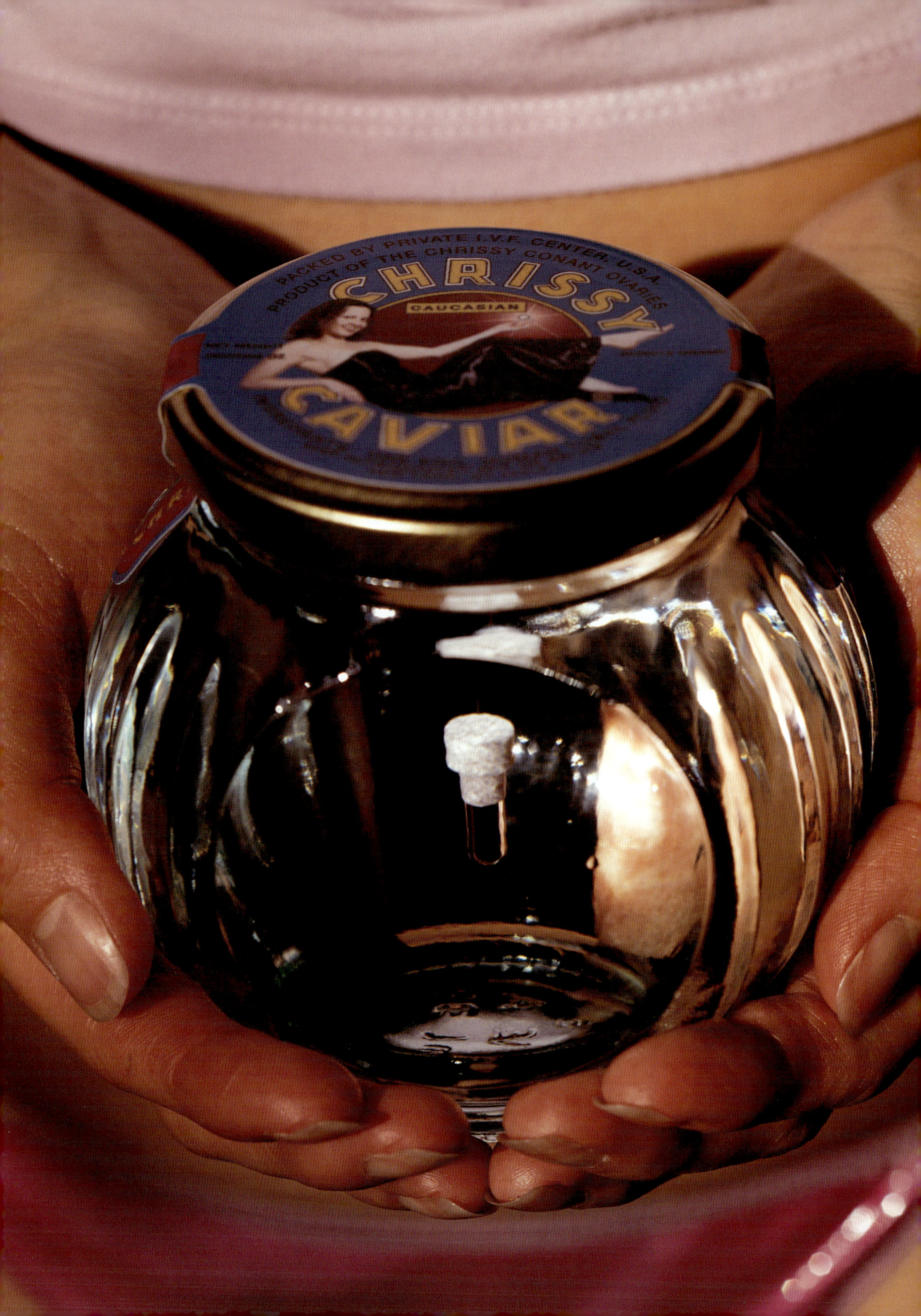

PACKED BY PRIVATE I.V.F. CENTER, U.S.A.
PRODUCT OF THE CHRISSY CONANT OVARIES
CHRISSY
CAUCASIAN
CAVIAR

Our families—eccentric or mainstream, supportive or trying, present or absent—define in large part who we are. Whether resolving conflicts, caring for ill parents, or committing to a life partner, we are constantly negotiating relationships to maintain the family unit in one form or another. Over time, the idea of what defines a family may have changed, but our dependence on it has not. These intimate and complex relationships impact our character and the decisions we make about our lives.

Artists navigate the same waters we all do. *Family* is composed of the work of thirty-seven artists who have made objects or images that reflect on the idea of family. The works could be thought of as falling into one of several categories: building a family, maintaining a family, or making sense of a family. Although certain works in the exhibition may be surprising for the honesty and boldness with which they are made, they do not reveal anything particularly exotic or surprising about family life. Rather, the works in this exhibition reflect certain conditions and observations—good and bad—of the contemporary, and, for that matter, the timeless, family.

Building a family

Perhaps it has always been hard to find the right mate and build the family you imagine. Chrissy Conant's *Chrissy Caviar* gives that pursuit a 2002 spin. For this work, Conant had a dozen of her eggs harvested by an embryologist, sealed into tiny tubes filled with human tubal fluid, and then packaged as caviar. The label on the jar essentially advertises her as, simultaneously, an eligible mate, object of desire, and producer of a delicacy. She writes, "I am trying to manifest, and be productive with, my highly emotional desires to find a Mr. Right, and create a family together." Despite advances in medical technology, women waiting to have children are still heavily impacted by their age. *Chrissy Caviar* gives this very private fear a public form. Rather than wait passively to be approached by a man, Conant's sculpture is an individual marketing strategy to connect herself with a mate. She uses all of the devices of the commercial sphere that are so familiar in American culture, including slick packaging, using sex to sell, and the suggestion of a limited quantity.

Patricia Cronin has created not just a sculpture, but a monument, to commemorate her relationship with her partner. The form the work takes is inspired by mortuary sculptures of the eighteenth and nineteenth centuries that depict full-length portraits of the deceased carved in marble. Cronin's *Memorial to a Marriage* depicts her sleeping with her partner in a loving embrace. The bodies of the two women are draped with a sheet that falls into elegant folds, recalling the elaborate drapery that sculptors throughout time have indulged not only for the way it demonstrates their skill, but also for its abstract beauty. Cronin's ambitious sculpture celebrates and makes official in death her "marriage," which cannot be made legal in life.

Chrissy Conant
Chrissy Caviar

(view of the artist holding sculptural component), 2001-02

Human eggs, human tubal fluid, liquid silicone, polyethyline, nylon, glass, brass, refrigeration equipment
52 x 49 x 47
Courtesy of the artist

Maintaining a family

Much of family life is quite mundane—shopping, eating, potty training.
Jonathan Seliger is adept at translating mundane objects of daily life into
larger metaphors. *For A Family* (1995-96) appears to be five pizza boxes
stacked on a table. The sculpture is in fact made from folded canvas, skillfully
painted to mimic cheap cardboard. The sculpture immediately starts us
guessing about the family it describes. A big family, maybe? Five eight-slice
pizzas, allowing three pieces per person, could feed thirteen people.
From the topping selection, we might be led to believe that there are not too
many little kids, since they're not likely to eat anchovies or mushrooms.
The sculpture might be thought of as a family portrait in food—a family
reduced to what it eats. Seliger's sculptures can be read as both telling
artifacts of contemporary life, and still life paintings, where ordinary objects
take on poetic meaning.

Tatsumi Orimoto's and Sophie Calle's photographs both document
difficult realities of their daily lives, although not in ways we are accustomed
to seeing the family recorded. Orimoto's often humorous, posed photographs
are in large part a strategy in the day to day struggle to both entertain and
stay engaged with his ailing mother. When making his mother smile became
increasingly challenging and increasingly necessary, Orimoto began bringing
empty cardboard boxes and discarded automobile tires on visits to use as
absurd props. His work is an example of the way in which art can sometimes
respond directly to life. It also captures the ambitious efforts of a devoted son
and the importance of play and humor in daily life.

Sophie Calle's *Autobiographies (The Rival)* reveals a horrible moment in
the artist's marriage. On finding a love letter her husband wrote to another
woman, "H," she scratched out the woman's initial and wrote in her own. She
made other alterations to the letter, irrationally editing it as if trying to make
improvements. Blowing the letter up to almost six feet high is probably no
exaggeration of the impact it had on her. The artifact writ large is a painfully
revealing snapshot of a marriage in crisis.

Making sense of a family

Alan Berliner's film about his father, titled *Nobody's Business*, introduces us
to a father and son who are emotionally close, but are having difficulty
understanding each other's lives. The film begins with Berliner's father
resisting the idea that his own personal history has any importance. The senior
Berliner says, "I'm just an ordinary guy who's lived an ordinary life... My life is
nothing." The film highlights the relationship between adult child and parent,
and the way in which generations differ in attitudes about personal history
and identity. Unlike his father, Berliner feels compelled to come to terms with
who his father is and make sense of the decisions he made about his life.

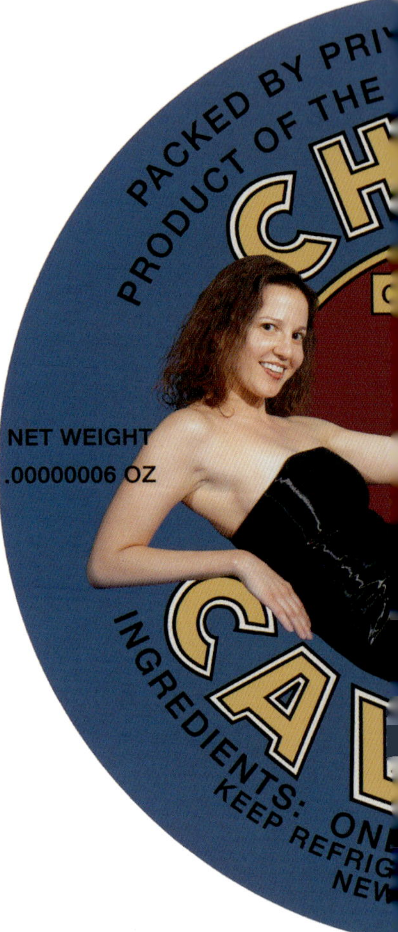

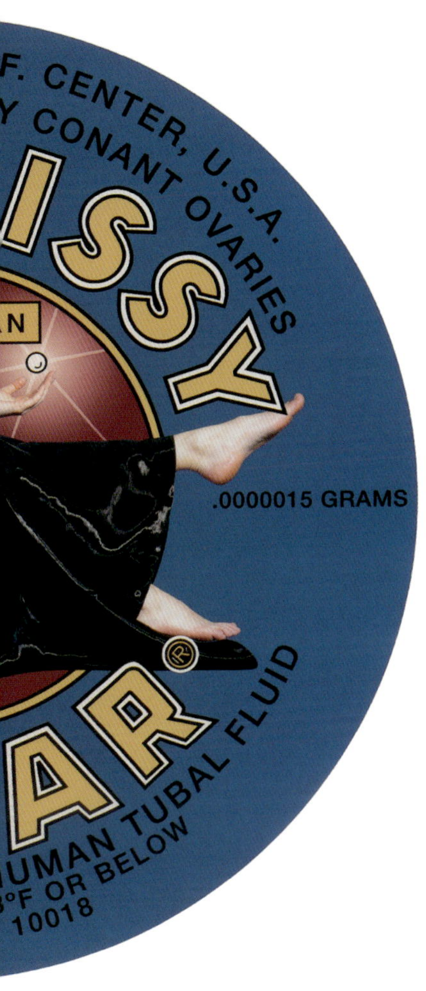

Chrissy Conant
Chrissy Caviar, 2001-02

Giclée print, #1/100
33 x 23 1/2
Courtesy of the artist

Robert Melee has created a body of work about his wildly eccentric mother and his relationship with her. *Mommy and Me* is a collection of family photos taken over the years, matted, framed together and covered in a yellow, plastic sheath reminiscent of tacky, protective sofa covers. While there are a few rather ordinary snapshots of mother and son, others are shockingly strange. His mother appears to be everything the stereotypical mother figure is not: she is sexual; she is altered dramatically with makeup and wigs; and she dresses provocatively, giving the viewer a sense that this is not an ordinary mother/son relationship. Melee's work expands the notion of what the supposed nurturer and pillar of family can look like. Melee's *Mommy and Me* frames and packages this eccentric life into manageable form.

In American culture we have a particularly heightened sense of the "normal family"—how they look and how they act. This idea is largely communicated (some might argue "marketed") through television. While the idea of what is normal has changed with the times, we still often compare our own home lives with the more glamorous, interesting, or stimulating ones we watch for entertainment. Mark Bennett's hilariously detailed architectural plans of the fictitious homes of famous television families make the lives of these characters more real, while at the same time making us more acutely aware of our absurd level of involvement with them.

For the British (and Anglophiles around the globe), the royal family provides another point of comparison to our own lives. Perhaps the original inspiration for reality television, the royals, who historically have been a source of envy, in recent times have made us happy to be commoners. While tragic drama after tragic drama unfolds in the media, it has become increasingly clear that the royals, despite efforts to protect their image, are as flawed as the rest of us. In Mark Wallinger's *Royal Ascot*, footage from four years of the procession as the royal family arrives at the famous horse races is played on four monitors. The stilted and routine pageantry is exaggerated through repetition. Each year's footage is remarkably similar. The family members more closely resemble a clip from a BBC miniseries than the dynasty whose tribulations have been made so public.

Whether king or commoner, our ability to adequately respond to, resist, or accept our families and their needs is in many ways the foundation upon which our characters are built. Tied to us by bonds of blood or solemn promise, love or hate, habit or shared experiences, they are our proscribed challenge—a certain set of qualities or circumstances to which we must rise. It is impossible not to reflect on our own families and relationships when looking at the works of art in this exhibition. Although highly personal, much of the artwork in *Family* also reveals universal and timeless truths about the family relationships we want so much to perfect.

Jessica Hough, *Associate Curator*

White Blouse White Shirt

Snow falls on the boardwalk
   where they never walked that winter,
streetlamps in white boas, surf light
   patching shuttered storefronts.
Where are they? The Ferris wheel
   they once rode looks green.

In this other snapshot
   she wears pedal pushers,
he's in summer whites,
   they swing cigarettes
and hold hands, walking toward me,
   it seems, into breezy life,
where they don't know I'm waiting.
   Now they're renting a rolling chair.
Inside the wicker cowl he says
   "A five-dollar ride, chief."
"It's Chinese, like Charlie Chan."
   Sand buries the sea noise,
resin scents rise from the boards
   into deft sea winds
as they roll past windows larvaed
   with delftware and sable stoles,
licking each other's fingers,
   french fries in paper cones.

When did the boardwalk look like that?
   When was that fresh love?
I stencil red-winged blackbirds
   into the scenes, and lilac
brushing windowpanes, and crocus,
   one garden of one season,
composite, where we look out,
   and between them I become
an hourglass of sand and light
   beside the ocean,
where the sun lets more snow
   fall around our heads.

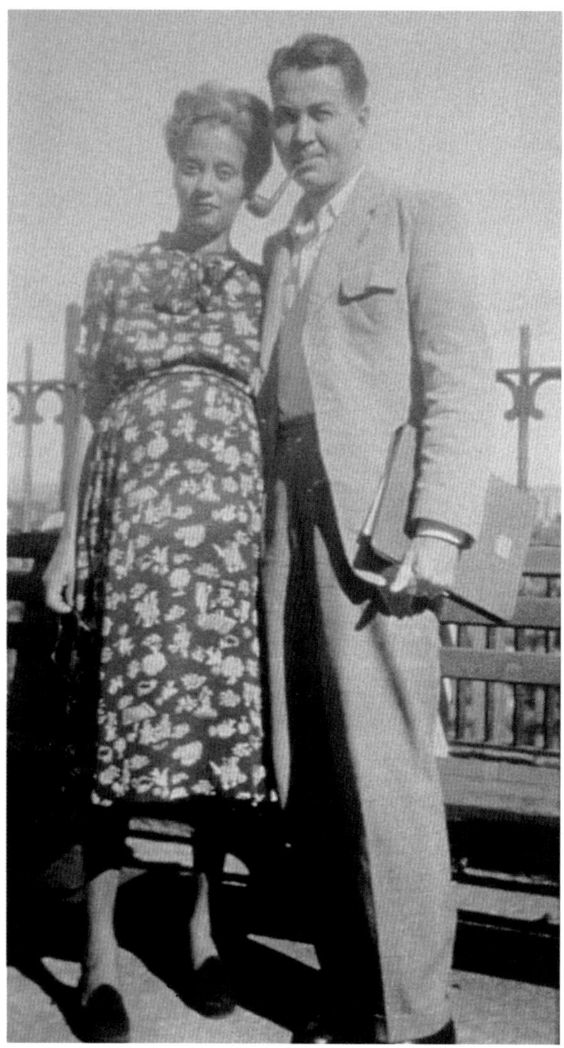

Adrian Piper
Ashes to Ashes, 1995

Photo-text work including:
   black and white photograph, 48 x 30
   text panel, 48 x 24
   color photograph, 18 x 30
   color photograph, 24 x 30
Collection of the artist

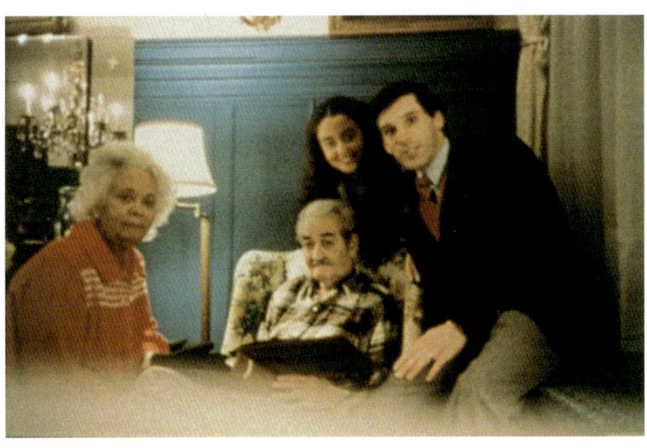

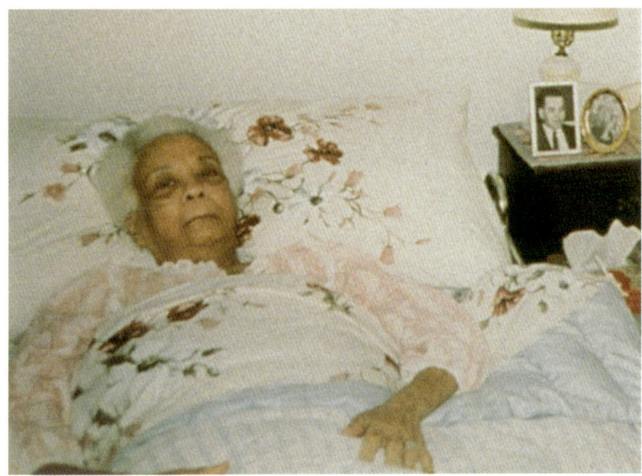

Following Page
Alan Berliner
Nobody's Business, 1996

Promotional photograph for 16mm film
converted to DVD, color, sound; 60 minutes
Courtesy of the artist

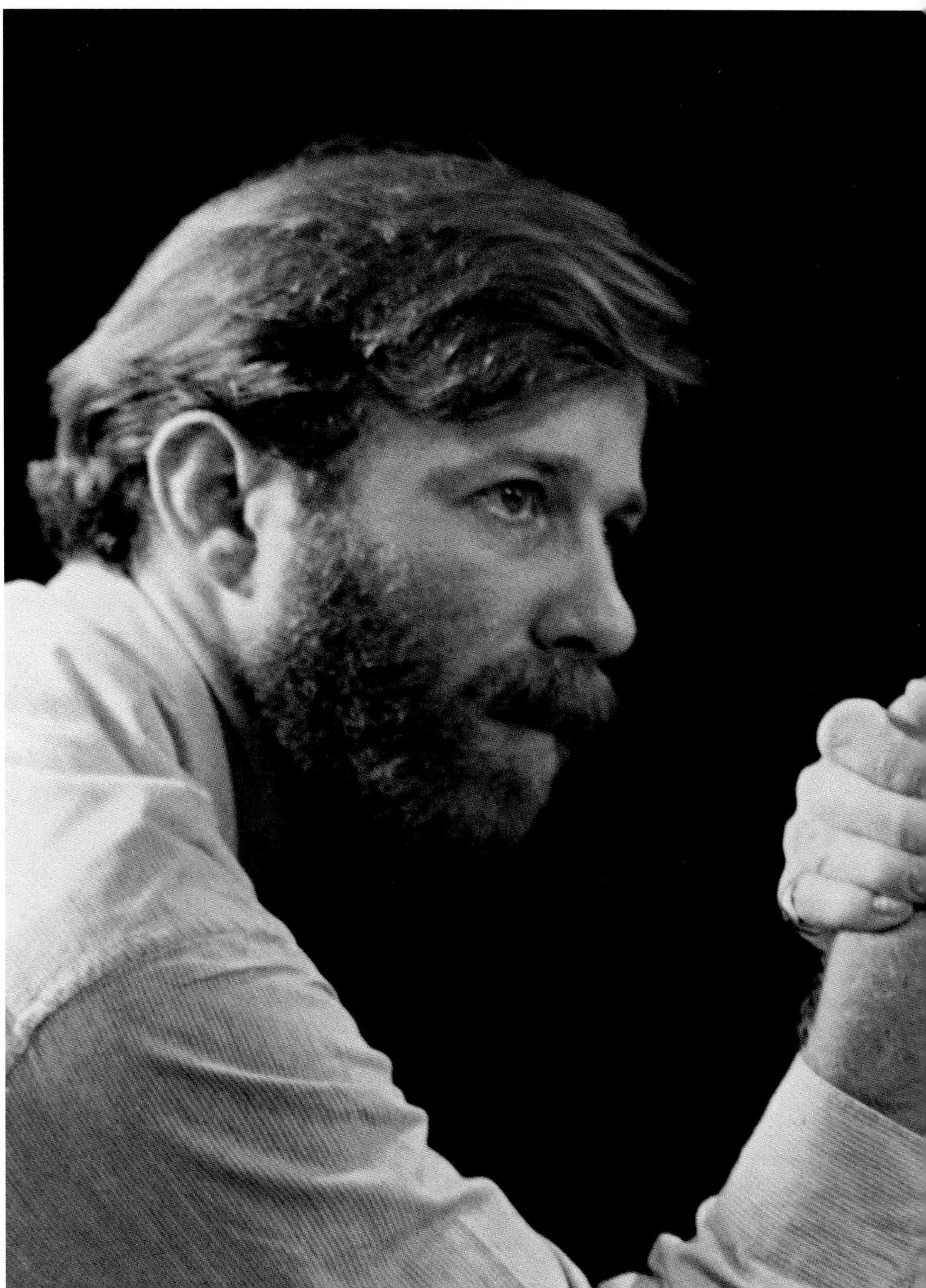

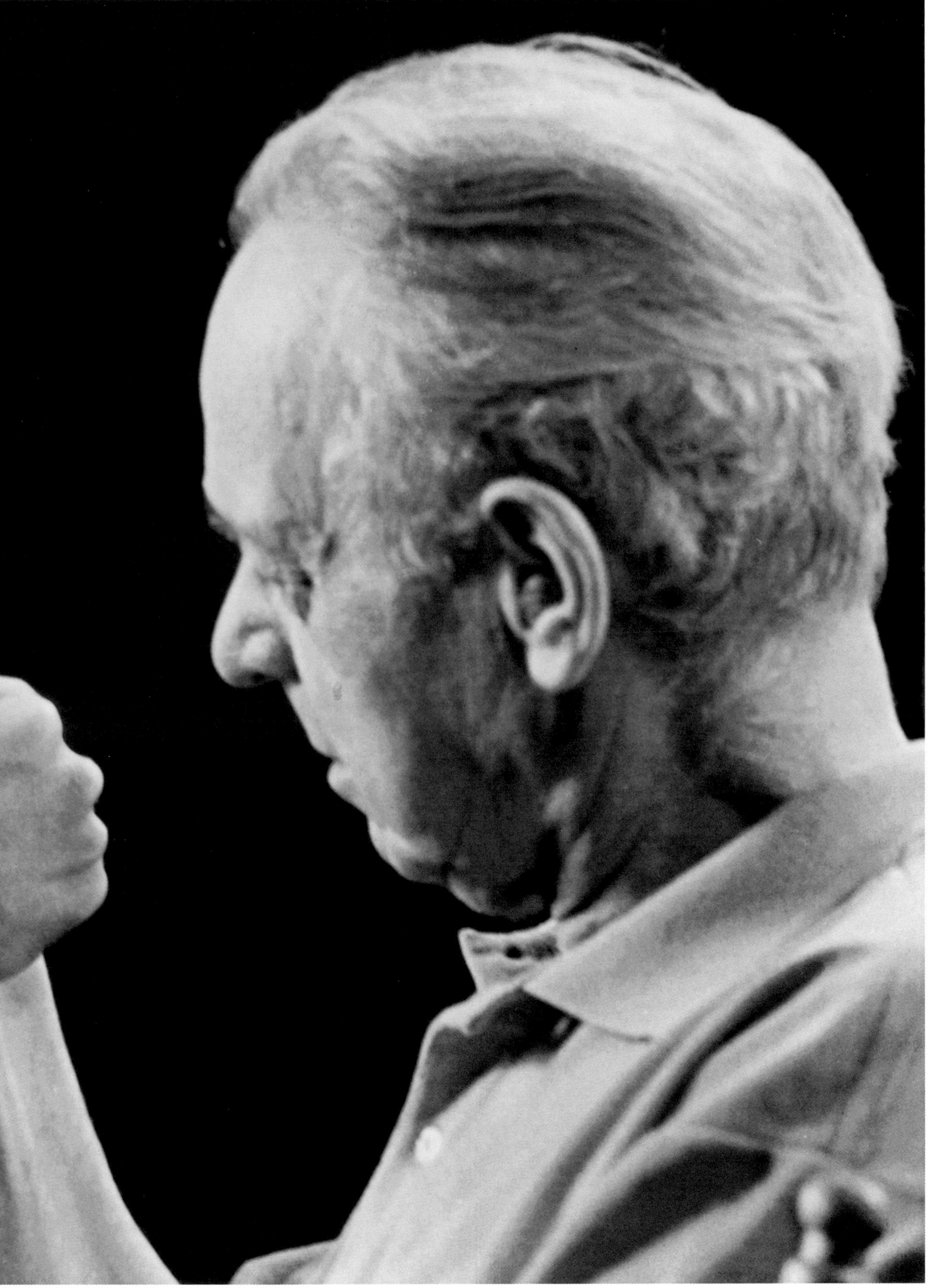

Robert Hass

My Mother's Nipples

They're where all displacement begins.
They bulldozed the upper meadow at Squaw Valley,
where horses from the stable, two chestnuts, one white,
grazed in the mist and the scent of wet grass on summer mornings
and moonrise threw the owl's shadow on voles and wood rats
crouched in the sage smell the earth gave back after dark
with the day's heat to the night air.
And after the framers began to pound nails
and the electricians and plumbers came around to talk specs
with the general contractor, someone put up the green sign
with alpine daisies on it that said Squaw Valley Meadows.
They had gouged up the deep-rooted bunchgrass
and the wet alkali-scented earth had been pushed aside
or trucked someplace out of the way, and they poured concrete
and laid road—pleasant scent of tar in the spring sun—

"He wanted to get out of his head," she said,
"so I told him to write about his mother's nipples."

The cosmopolitan's song on this subject:

Alors! les nipples de ma mère!

The romantic's song

What could be more fair
than les nipples de ma mère?

The utopian's song

I will freely share
les nipples de ma mère.

The philosopher's song

Here was always there
with les nipples de ma mère

The capitalist's song

Fifty cents a share

The saint's song

Lift your eyes in prayer

The misanthrope's song

I can scarcely bear

The melancholic's song

They were never there,
les nipples de ma mère.
They are not anywhere.

The indigenist's song

And so the boy they called Loves His Mother's Tits
Went into the mountains and fasted for three days.
On the fourth he saw a red-tailed hawk with broken wings,
On the fifth a gored doe in a ravine, entrails
Spilled onto the rocks, eye looking up at him
From the twisted neck. All the sixth day he was dizzy
And his stomach hurt. On the seventh he made three deep cuts
In the meat of his palm. He entered the pain at noon
And an eagle came to him crying three times like the mewling
A doe makes planting her hooves in the soft duff for mating
And he went home and they called him Eagle Three Times after
   that.

The regionalist's song

Los Pechos.
Rolling oak woodland between Sierra pines
and the simmering valley.

Pink, of course, soft; a girl's—
She wore white muslin tennis outfits
in the style Helen Wills made fashionable.
Trim athletic swimsuits.
A small person, compact body. In the photographs
she's on the beach, standing straight,
hands on hips, grinning,
eyes desperate even then.

Mothers in the nineteen forties didn't nurse.
I never saw her naked. Oh! yes, I did,
once, but I can't remember. I remember
not wanting to.

Two memories. My mother had been drinking for several days, and I had thought dinner would be cancelled, so I wouldn't get to watch *The Lone Ranger* on my aunt's and uncle's television set. But we went to dinner and my aunt with her high-pitched voice took the high-minded tone that she took in my mother's presence. She had put out hard candies in little cut glass dishes as she always did, and we ate dinner, at which water was served to the grown-ups, and no one spoke except my uncle who teased us in his English accent. A tall man. He used to pat me on the head too hard and say, "Robert of Sicily, brother of the Pope Urbane." And after dinner when the television was turned on in the immaculate living room and Silver was running across the snowy screen, his mane shuddering from the speed, the door bell rang. It was two men in white coats and my mother bolted from the table into the kitchen and out the back door. The men went in after her. The back stairs led into a sort of well between the houses, and when I went into the kitchen I could hear her screaming, "No! no!," the sound echoing and re-echoing among the houses.

Some years later. I am perhaps ten, eleven. We are visiting my mother on the parklike grounds of the State Hospital in the Napa Valley. It is Sunday again. Green lawns, the heavy sweet scent of mock orange. Many of the patients are walking, alone or with their families, on the paths. One man seemed to be giving speeches to a tree. I had asked my grandmother why, if my mother had a drinking problem, that's the phrase I had been taught to use, why she was locked up with crazy people. It was a question I could have asked my father, but I understood that his answer would not be dependable. My grandmother said, with force, she had small red curls on her forehead, dressed with great style, you had better ask your father that. Then she thought better of it, and said, They have a treatment program, dear, maybe it will help. I tried out that phrase, treatment program. My mother was sitting on a bench. She looked immensely sad, seemed to have shrunk. Her hair was pulled across her forehead and secured with a white beret, like Teresa Wright in the movies. At first my brother and I just sat next to her on the bench and cried. My father held my sister's hand. My grandmother and grandfather stood to one side, a separate group, and watched.

Later, while they talked, I studied a middle-aged woman sitting on the next bench talking to herself in a foreign language. She was wearing a floral print dress and she spoke almost in a whisper but with passion, looking around from time to time, quick little furtive resentful glances. She was so careless of herself that I could see her breast, the brown nipple, when she leaned forward. I didn't want to look, and looked, and looked away.

Hot Sierra morning.
Brenda working in another room.
Rumble of heavy equipment in the meadow,
bird squall, Steller's jay, and then
the piercing three-note whistle of a robin.
They're mating now. Otherwise they're mute.
Mother-ing. Or Mother-song.
Mother-song-song-song.

We used to laugh, my brother and I in college,
about the chocolate cake. Tears in our eyes laughing.
In grammar school, whenever she'd start to drink,
she panicked and made amends by baking chocolate cake.
And, of course, when we got home, we'd smell the strong, sweet
    smell
of the absolute darkness of chocolate,
and be too sick to eat it.

The first girl's breasts I saw
were the Chevy dealer's daughter Linda Wren's.
Pale in the moonlight. Little nubbins, pink-nosed.
I can still hear the slow sound of the surf
of my breath drawing in. I think I almost fainted.

Twin fonts of mercy, they used to say of the Virgin's breasts
in the old liturgy the Irish priests
could never quite handle, it being a form of bodily reference,
springs of grace, freshets
of lovingkindness. If I remember correctly,
there are baroque poems in this spirit
in which each of Christ's wounds is a nipple.
Drink and live: this is the son's blood.

Dried figs, candied roses.

What is one to say of the nipples of old women
who would, after all, find the subject
unseemly.

Yesterday I ran along the edge of the meadow in the heat
of late afternoon. So many wildflowers
tangled in the grass. So many grasses—
reedgrass, the bentgrass and timothy, little quaking grass,
dogtail, rip-gut brome—the seeds flaring from the stalks
in tight chevrons of green and purple-green
but loosening.

I said to myself:
some things do not blossom in this life.

I said: what we've lost is a story
and what we've never had
a song.

When my father died, I was curious to see in what ratio she would
feel relieved and lost. All during the days of his dying, she stood by
his bed talking to whichever of her children was present about the
food in the cafeteria or the native state of the nurses—"She's from
Portland, isn't that interesting? Your Aunt Nell lived in Portland
when Owen was working for the Fisheries."—and turn occasionally
to my father who was half-conscious, his eyes a morphine cloud, and
say, in a sort of baby talk, "It's all right, dear. It's all right." And after
he died, she was dazed, and clearly did not know herself whether
she felt relieved or lost, and I felt sorry for her that she had no habit
and so no means of self-knowing. She was waiting for us to leave so
she could start drinking. Only once was she suddenly alert. When
the young man from the undertaker's came and explained that she
would need a copy of her marriage license in order to do something
about the insurance and pensions, she looked briefly alive, anxious,
and I realized that, though she rarely told the truth, she was a very
poor dissembler. Now her eyes were a young girl's. What, she asked,
if someone just couldn't turn up a marriage license; it seemed such a
detail, there must be cases. I could see that she was trying out av-
enues of escape, and I was thinking, now what? They were never
married? I told her not to worry. I'd locate it. She considered this
and said it would be fine. I could see she had made some decision,
and then she grew indefinite again.
     So, back in California, it was with some interest that I retraced
the drive from San Francisco to Santa Rosa which my parents made
in 1939, when according to my mother's story—it was the first ac-
count of it I'd ever heard—she and my father had eloped. The
Sonoma County Office of Records was in a pink cinder-block building landscaped with reptilian pink oleanders which were still
blooming in the Indian summer heat. It would have been raining
when my parents drove that road in an old (I imagined) cream-
colored Packard convertible I had seen one photo of. I asked the
woman at the desk for the marriage certificate for February 1939. I
wondered what the surprise was going to be, and it was a small one.
No problem, Mrs. Minh said. But you had the date wrong, so it took
me a while to find it. It was October, not February. Driving back to
San Francisco, I had time to review this information. My brother
was born in December 1939. Hard to see that it meant anything except that my father had tried very hard to avoid his fate. I felt so
sorry for them. That they thought it was worth keeping a secret. Or,
more likely, that their life together began in a negotiation too painful
to be referred to again. That my mother had, with a certain fatality,
let me pick up the license, so her first son would not know the cir-

cumstance of his conception. I felt sorry for her shame, for my father's panic. It finished off my dim wish that there had been an early
romantic or ecstatic time in their lives, a blossoming, brief as a
northern summer maybe, but a blossoming.

What we've never had is a song
and what we've really had is a song.
Sweet smell of timothy in the meadow.
Clouds massing east above the ridge in a sky
as blue as the mountain lakes,
so there are places on this earth clear all the way up
and all the way down
and in between a various blossoming,
the many seed shapes of the many things
finding their way into flower or not,
that the wind scatters.

There are all kinds of emptiness and fullness
that sing and do not sing.

I said: you are her singing.

I came home from school and she was gone. I don't know what instinct sent me to the park. I suppose it was the only place I could
think of where someone might hide: she had passed out under an orange tree, curled up. Her face. flushed, eyelids swollen, was a ruin.
Though I needed urgently to know whatever was in it, I could
hardly bear to look. When I couldn't wake her, I decided to sit with
her until she woke up. I must have been ten years old: I suppose I
wanted for us to look like a son and mother who had been picnick-
ing, like a mother who had fallen asleep in the warm light and scent
of orange blossoms and a boy who was sitting beside her daydream-
ing, not thinking about anything in particular.

You are not her singing, though she is what's
broken in a song.
She is its silences.

She may be its silences.

Hawk drifting in the blue air,
grey of the granite ridges,
incense cedars, pines.

I tried to think of some place on earth she loved.

I remember she only ever spoke happily
of high school.

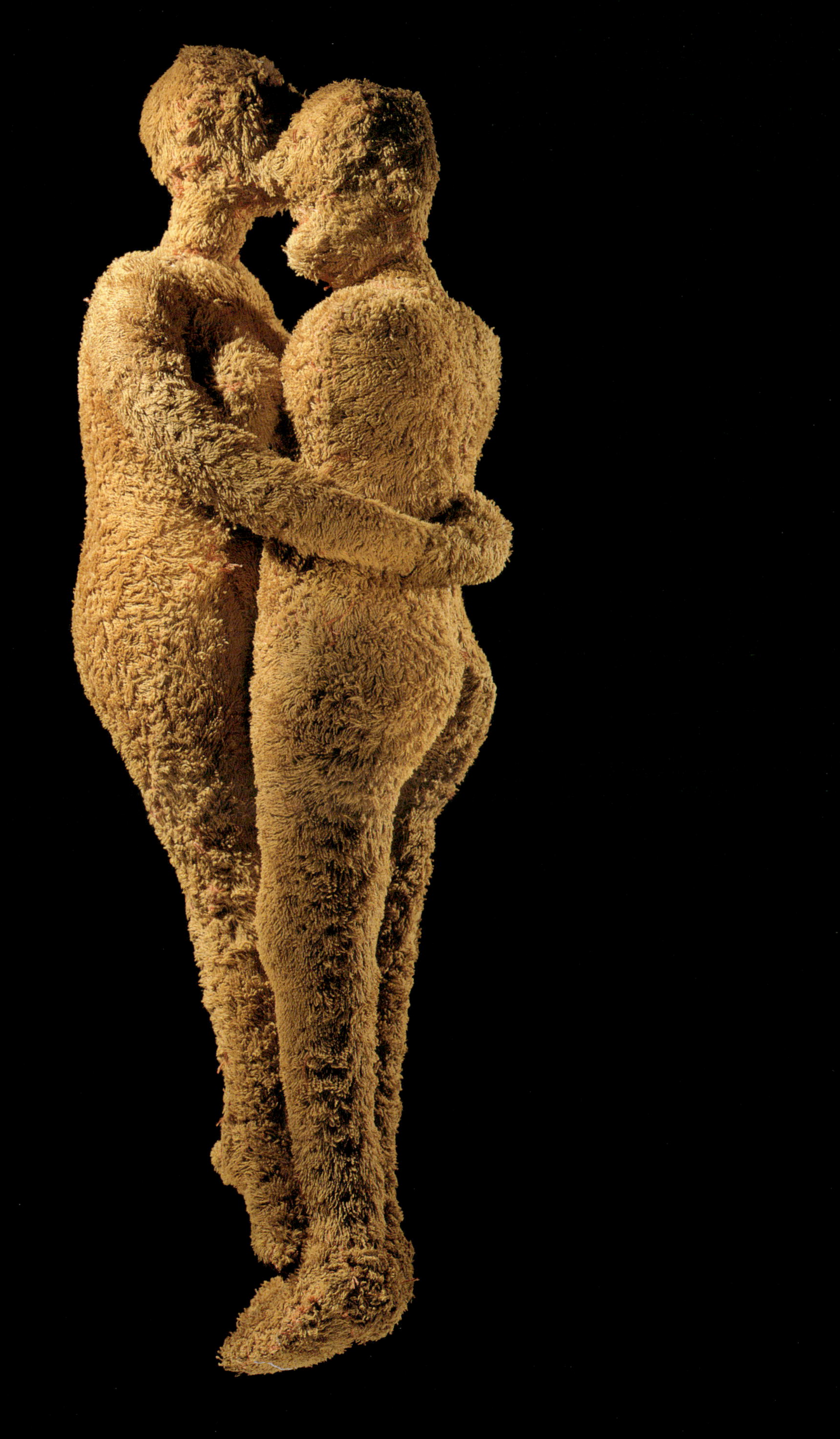

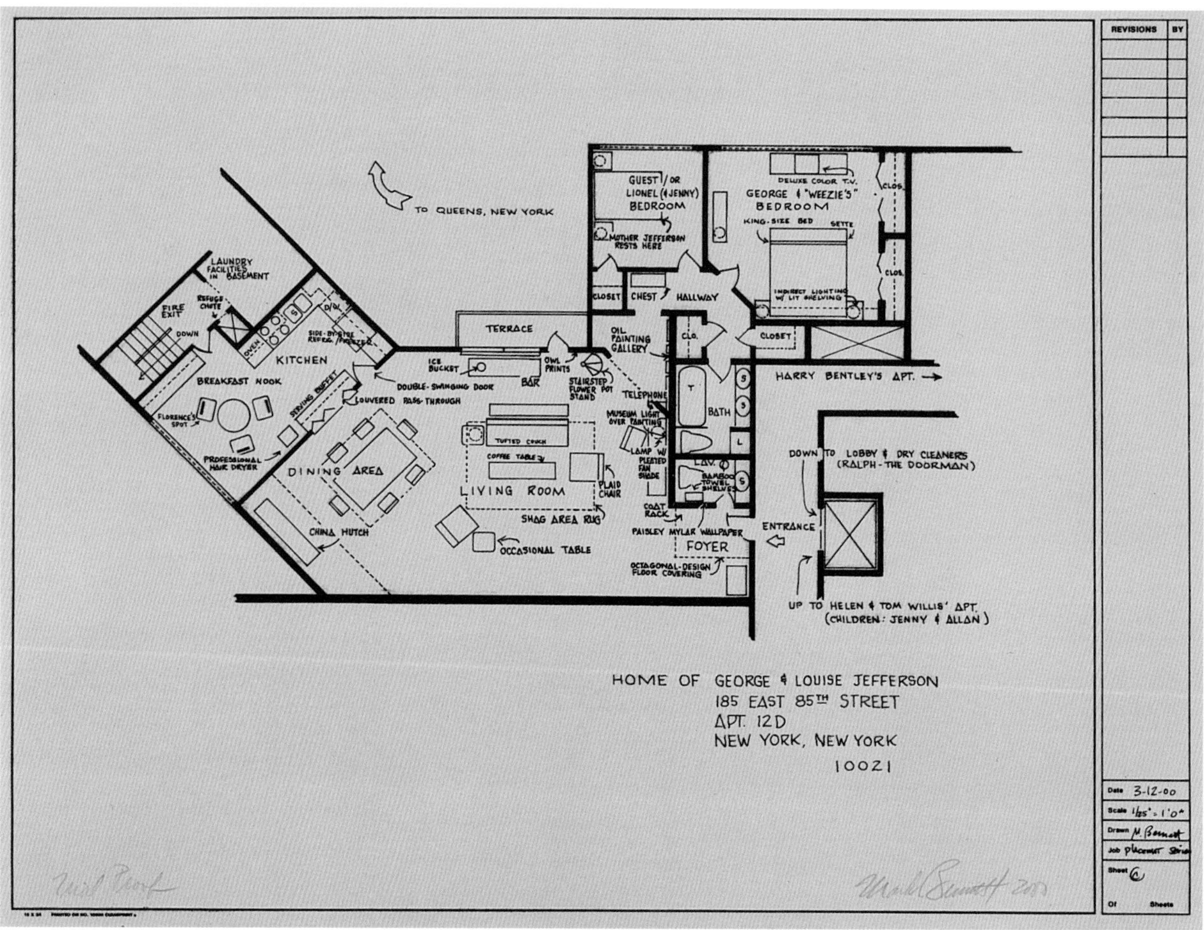

Preceding Page

Louise Bourgeois

Couple, 2001

Fabric
20 x 6 1/2
Courtesy of the artist
and Cheim & Read, New York

Mark Bennett

Home of: George and
Louise Jefferson, 2000

Etching
17 1/2 x 22 1/2 framed
Courtesy of the artist and the Mark Moore Gallery,
Santa Monica, CA

Following Page

Christoph Raitmayr

Ikea — Storage as a
Self-portrait, 2000

Wood
70 x 62 x 11
Courtesy of the artist and Galerie Krinzinger, Vienna

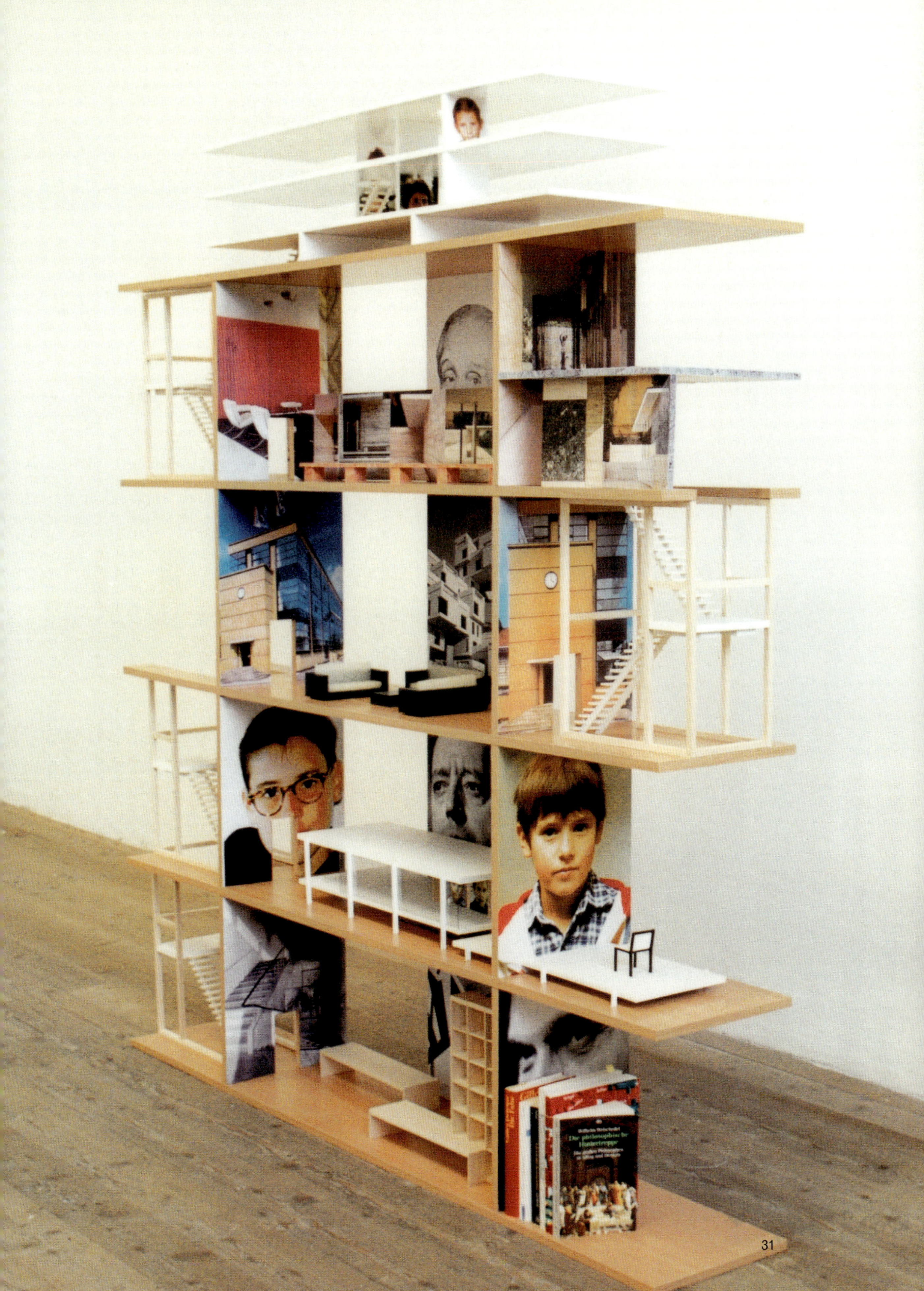

On Leaving My Son's Wedding Before the Cutting of the Cake

You were begotten in a wet field with flyaway dandelion hair.
Oh where was my straight-edged canvas, I can't paint a thing on the grass
except grass. I love you and the green grass rises. The grass
is taller than I am, ready to seed, quick under the brutal stars.
The grass grows golden through the middle of a fire. It burns.
My green my hay-dust my blackening star what I love is not mine and it burns.

In the church dressing-room you threaten to bush. To stick out
of the universe and bush. You're the white of rolling horse eyes
when the hay barn burns, *get a grip*. I go out and buy you Tums.
You lay yourself out on the tobacco-colored table, oh give
night a shove with your hayloft shoulder be man and grass,
be lion and rise up bridegroom rise up for your hour comes.

Tall and slender in your funereal sheath, you'd rescue Eurydice
from the fathers' clutches, though they've already stained
all things woman all things sweet and glad?
In this graying world, is nothing rad? Would you pick her
with your mushroom white hand, mushroom moist now would you pick her?
Are you lion-colored basket bee-colored swarm of vows?

And what am I to do, blow off with you in your rented red Corvette
into luscious miles, white hair flying? Pitch hay to your smoking wheels? For
        pete's
sake get up, they want your picture now, for pity's sake
show a tooth or two! What's this, an impatient jab? A son
grows through the middle of his dad, custom hot, incurable.
You brush skin-ash from my shoulders I am father again smoldering loved.

Look where your bride comes a walking gardenia cool and slow,
stepping stopping in measure up the aisle
on her father's choleric arm. How you look at her,
a look to douse the great fire's everlasting squabble. A look
how long kept up the sleeves of your heart out of the heat
when the family was crackling whining with fear and love?

One dark I knock on your new apartment door, my heart
kicking in its strangely hot stall. Your wife's lost her upswept hair,
she's just a girl. She winces as she cuts the cake I bring,
as if it might be somebody's child. I hug you hayloaf
through my fire-retardant coat and saying good-bye step out
under the fires whipped across the nothing of the night.

Sophie Calle

Autobiographies (The Rival), 1992

Silver gelatin print, text panel
86 x 38 1/4
Courtesy of the artist and Paula Cooper Gallery, New York

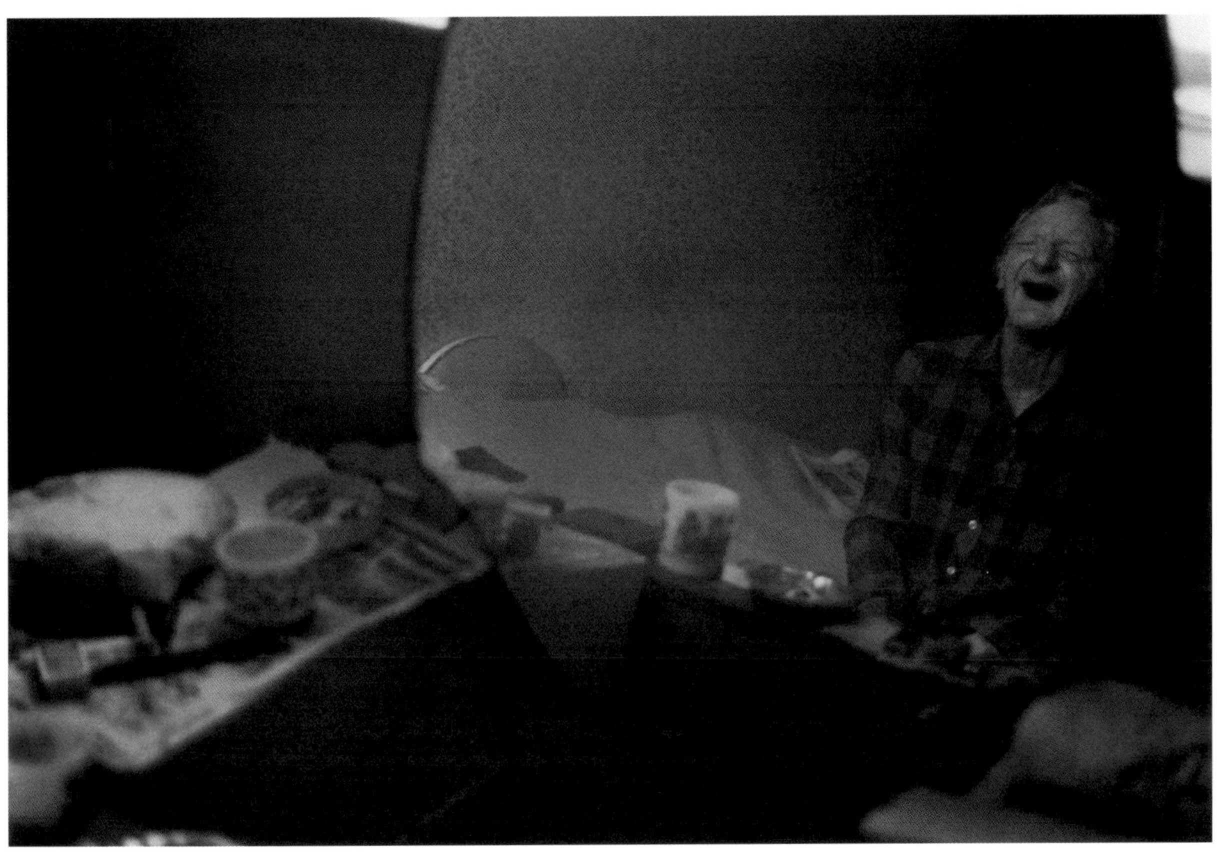

Richard Billingham
Untitled, 1991

Black and white print mounted on aluminum
38 1/2 x 58
Courtesy Anthony Reynolds Gallery, London

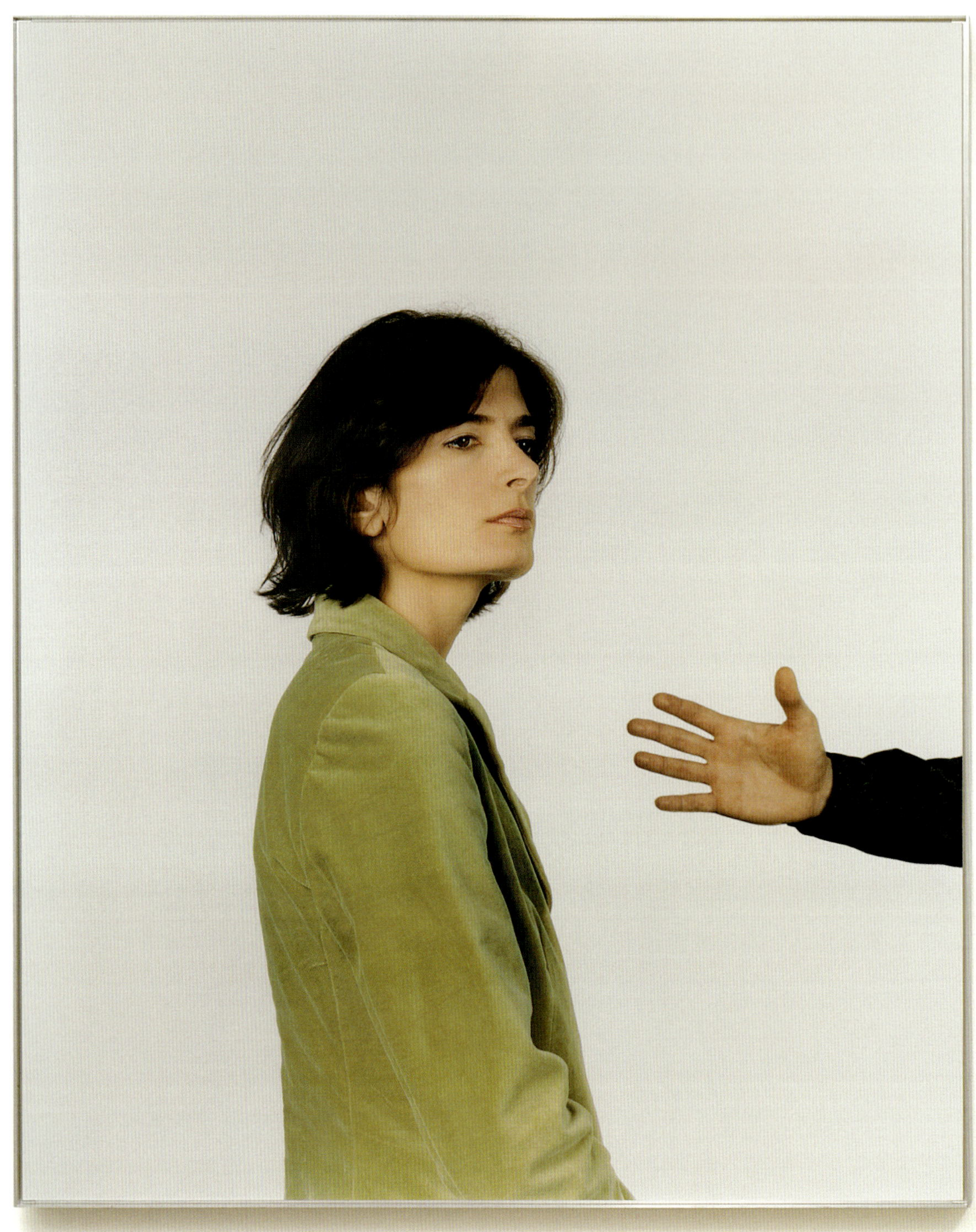

Geneviève Cadieux
Elle et Lui, 1997

Diptych; chromogenic print mounted on
Plexiglas with aluminum frame
77 1/2 x 62 1/2
The Bailey Collection, Toronto, Ontario

36

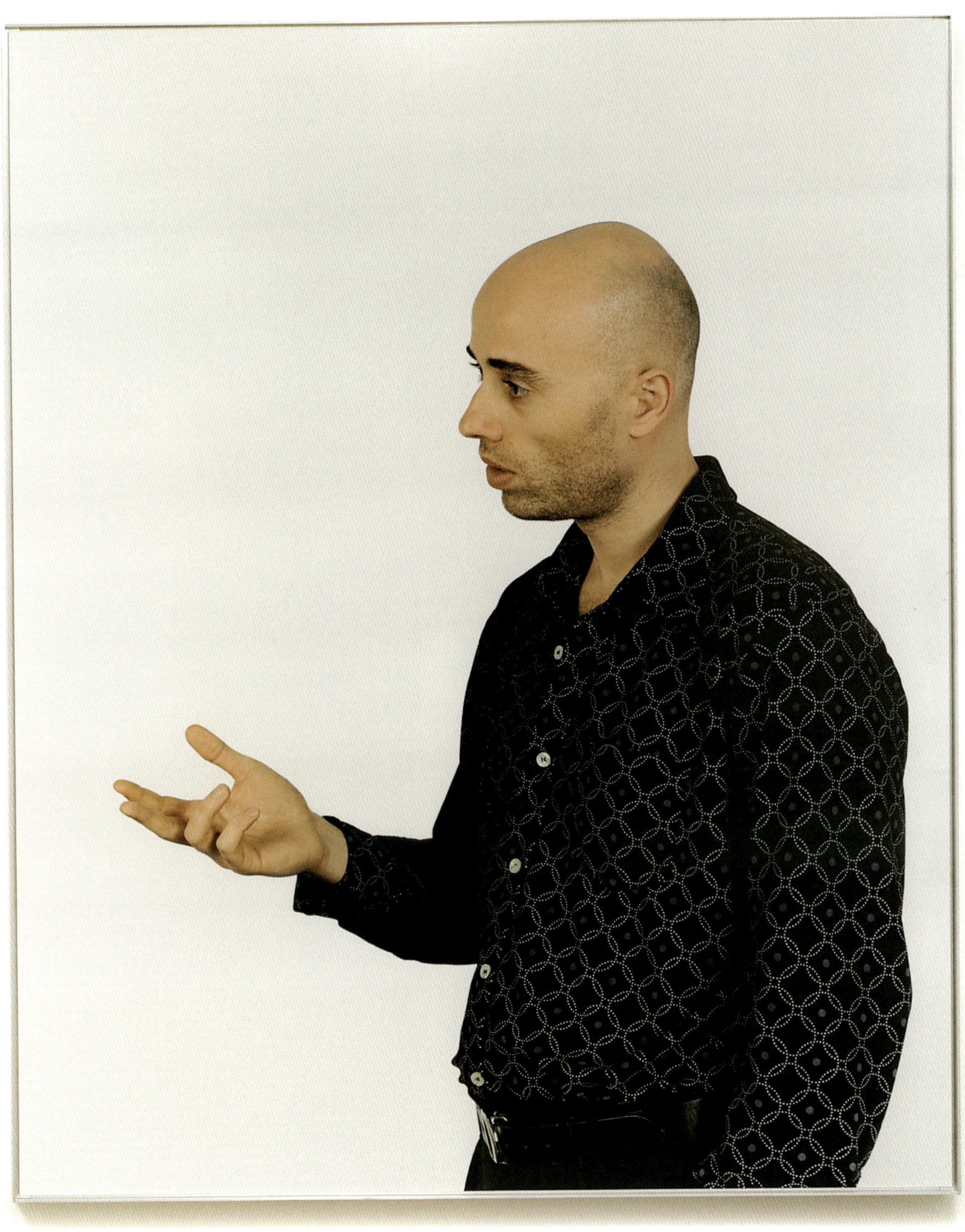

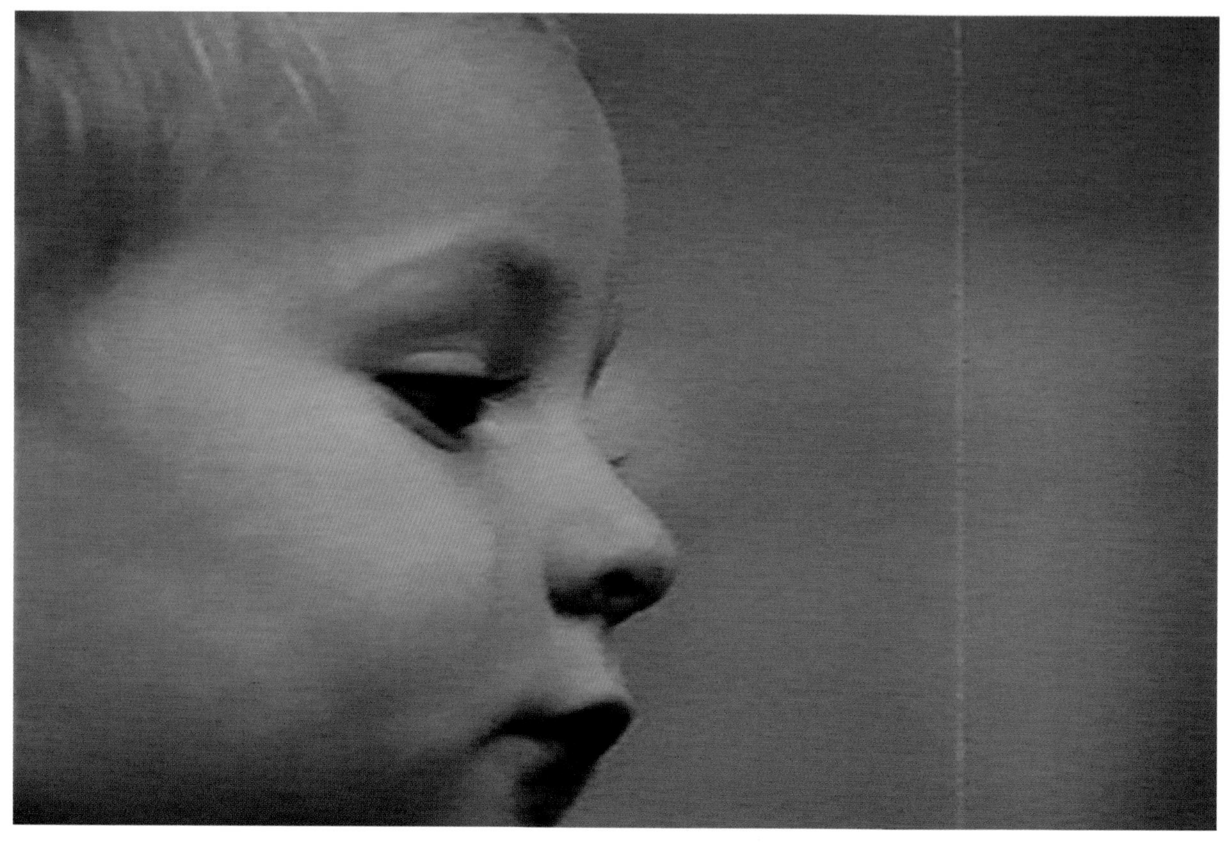

Laura Dunn
Baby (film still), 1999

16mm film converted to DVD;
black and white, sound, 5 minutes
Courtesy of the artist

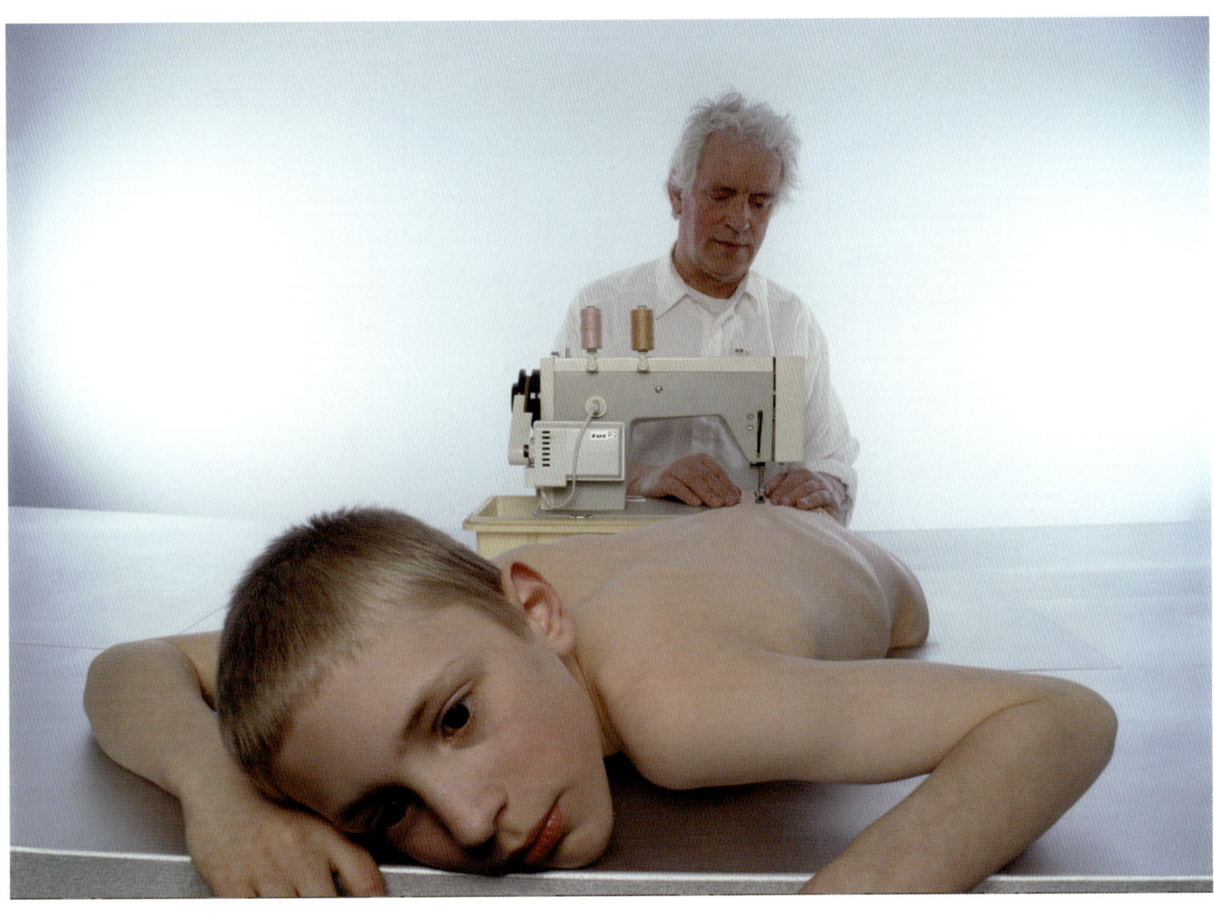

Margi Geerlinks
Pinocchio, 1999

Cibachrome print, Plexiglas, dibond
50 x 67
Collection of Ikkan Sanada, New York

Say You Love Me

What happened earlier I'm not sure of.
Of course he was drunk, but often he was.
His face looked like a ham on a hook above

me—I was pinned to the chair because
he'd hunkered over me with arms like jaws
pried open by the chair arms. "Do you love

me?" he began to sob. "Say you love me!"
I held out. I was probably fifteen.
What had happened? Had my mother—had she

said or done something? Or had he just been
drinking too long after work? "He'll get *mean*, "
my sister hissed, "just *tell* him." I brought my knee

up to kick him, but was too scared. Nothing
could have got the words out of me then. Rage
shut me up, yet "DO YOU?" was beginning

to peel, as of live layers of skin, age
from age from age from him until he gazed
through hysteria as a wet baby thing

repeating, "Do you love me? Say you do,"
in baby chokes, only loud, for they came
from a man. There wouldn't be a rescue

from my mother, still at work. The same
choking sobs said, "Love me, love me," and my game
was breaking down because I couldn't do

anything, not escape into my own
refusal, *I won't, I won't*, not fantasize
a kind, rich father, not fill the narrowed zone,

empty except for confusion until the size
of my fear ballooned as I saw his eyes,
blurred, taurean—my sister screamed—unknown,

unknown to me, a voice rose and leveled
off, "I love you," I said. "*Say 'I love you,
Dad!'*" "I love you, Dad," I whispered, leveled

by defeat into a cardboard image, untrue,
unbending. I was surprised I could move
as I did to get up, but he stayed, burled

onto the chair—my monstrous fear—she screamed,
my sister, "Dad, the phone! Go answer it!"
The phone wasn't ringing, yet he seemed

to move toward it, and I ran. He had a fit—
"It's not ringing!—but I was at the edge of it
as he collapsed into the chair and blamed

both of us at a distance. No, the phone
was not ringing. There was no world out there,
so there we remained, completely alone.

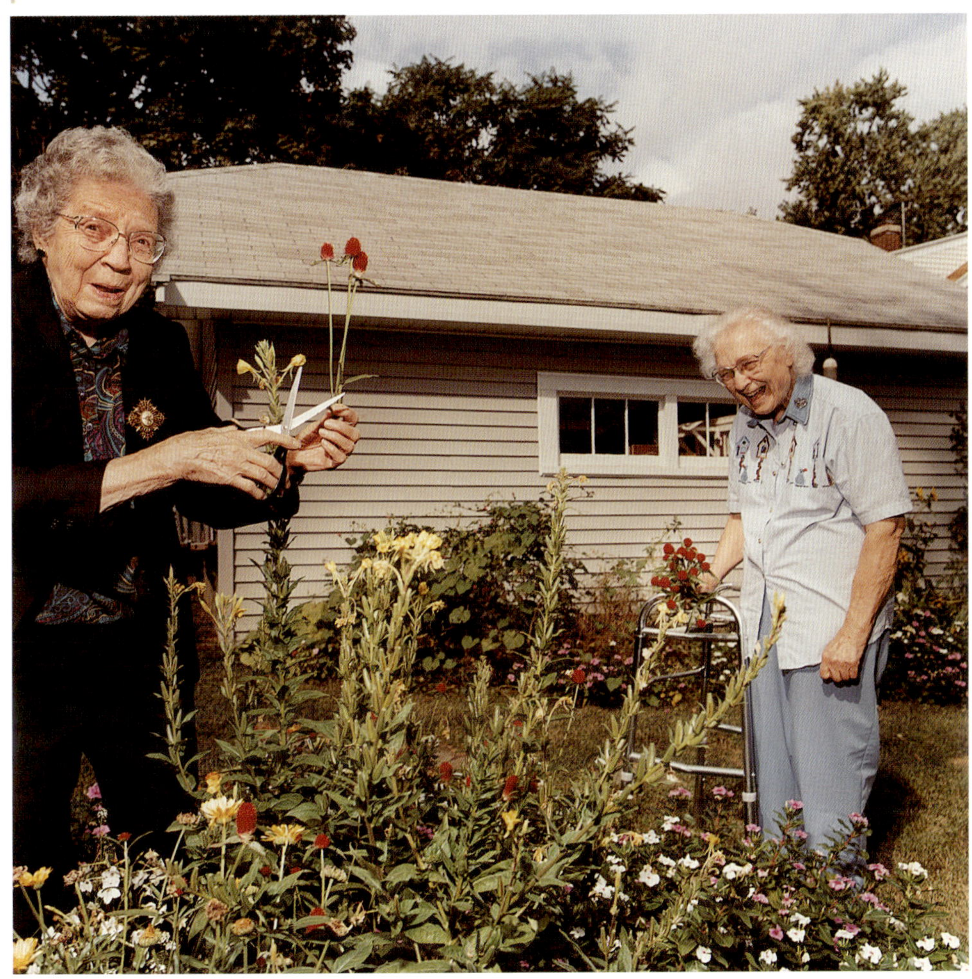

Chris Verene
Untitled (Galesburg #51), 2000

Chromogenic print
24 x 20
Courtesy of the artist and Paul Morris Gallery, New York

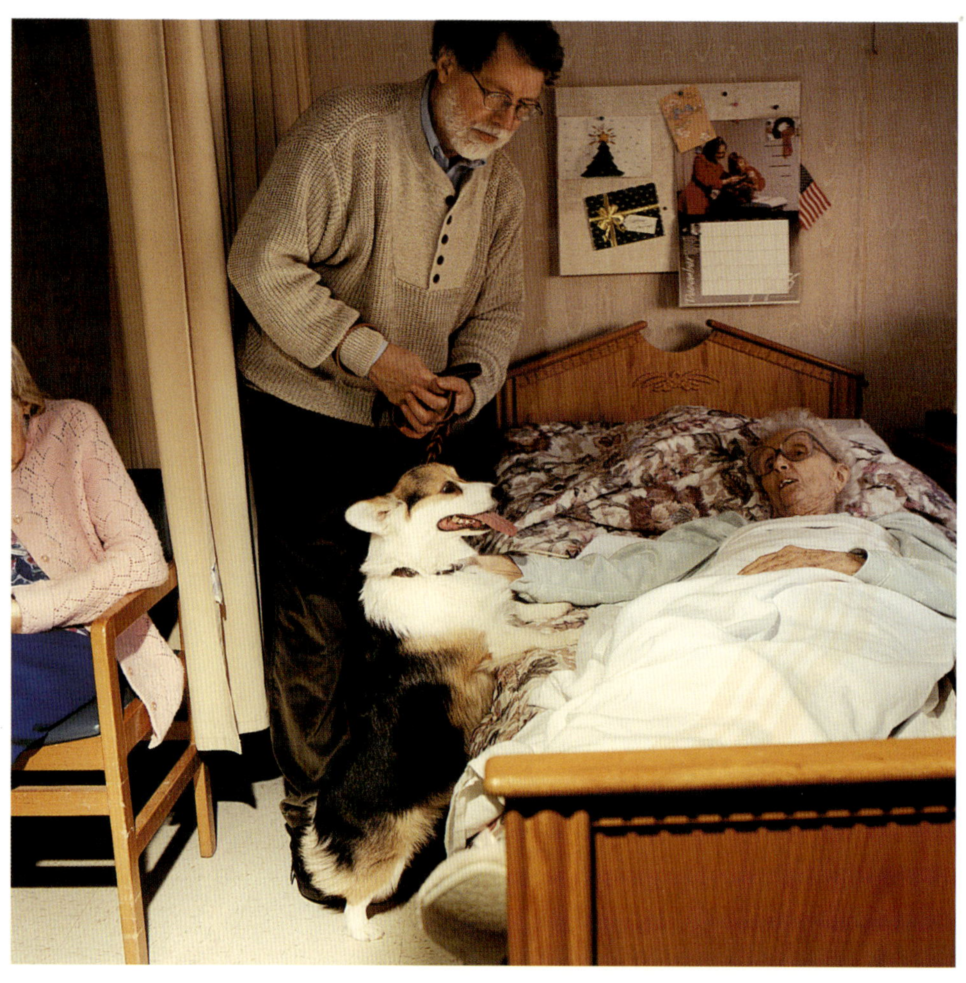

Chris Verene
Untitled (Galesburg #58), 1999-2000

Chromogenic print
24 x 20
Courtesy of the artist and Paul Morris Gallery, New York

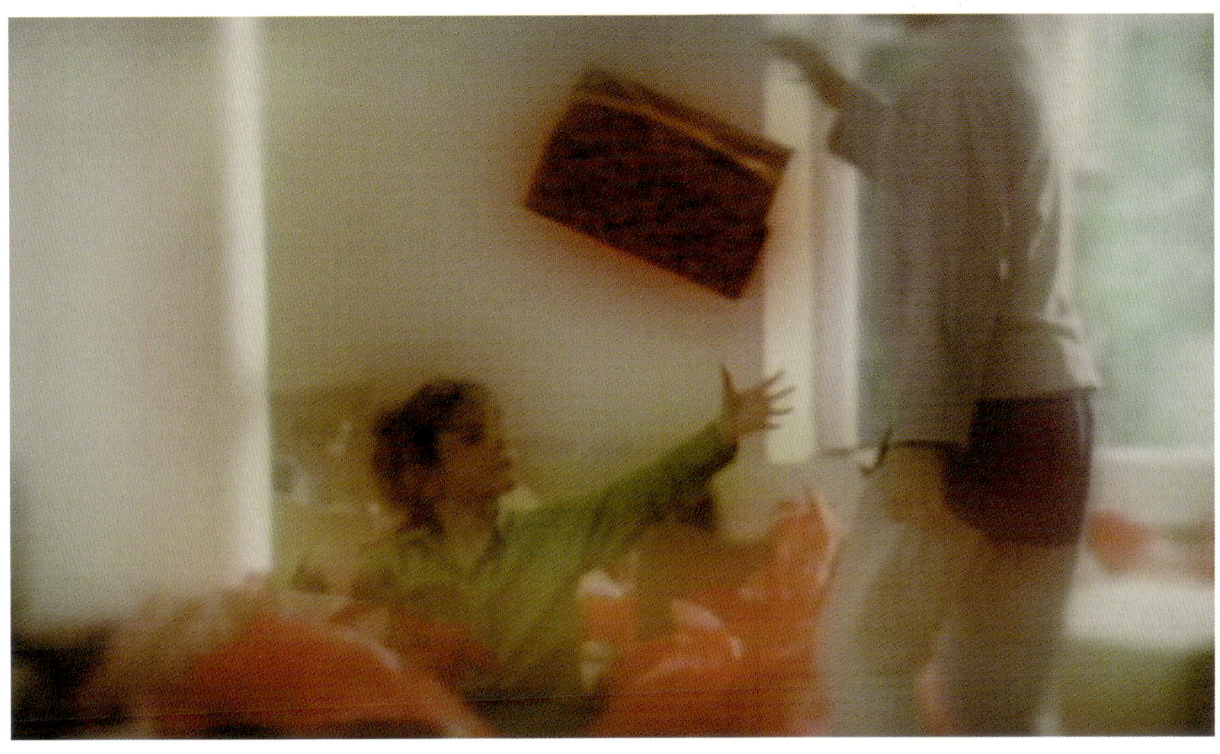

Maria Marshall
President Bill Clinton, Memphis,
Tennessee, November 13, 1993 (video still), 2000

DVD projection; color, sound, 1:23 minute loop
Courtesy of the artist and Team Gallery, New York

(the voice can stop horizontally)

Two Brothers

I have doubted my belief in sentences because of their
        refusal to recall certain things.

A way of being satisfied. A sound.

So the wish to restore them "arose"—

Walking with two brothers down Copacabana in the fifties
        city of gold teeth *açucar* such nerves,

a developing time sandwich holding hands on the black and
        white sidewalk, wavy like the graph of a patient who
        has not been born yet,—

our six feet shuffling through childhood my brothers' sea babble
        delicious remedy keeping me mixed with them;

Love comes from nothing but it comes.

Maybe it's not that day but near it; a loose agitated brightness
        that needs rescuing...

The spirits will work anywhere: past the vanilla courtyards'
        foam, sound flies, shells of grub cravings;

each word makes an outline come out of the body.

"To think" means: the looseness is taken away.

allvonnish *adj* [Baumgardner family word; < PennDu *allvannish*, prob < Ger *alle*, all + Ger *Wahnsinn*, craziness; curr bef 1900-] **1.** really mixed up; crazy; not in one's right mind **2.** lazy; having no incentive or ambition

> **1944** This was a crazy and lazy day Savilla was to the Dr's for a treatment - and Maggie is so allvanish it was late when she got there so Bessie had to help Mother with the dinner. {Hen & Chick Club Minutes, Margaret Eplett recording, 20 Apr}

bagtree *n* [Nancy Huth's word; < bag (the "fruit") + tree (the plant); curr 1994-] a tree with plastic grocery bags entangled in its branches

> **1996** The bagtrees are in bloom. {Nancy to Geof Huth, conv, Apr}

cousies *n* [Geof Huth's word; < Cous-Cous (our prairie dog) + cooties (imaginary infective quality children believe is transmitted by members of the opposite sex); curr 1995-] the smell of our prairie dog, Cous-Cous, which would drive our dogs crazy with hunting instinct

> **1996** "You know, Duck's following me around." "It's because you have cousies." {Erin & Nancy Huth, conv, 2 May}

daynights *n* [Erin Huth's word; < her misconstruing of the *light* of *daylights* w/ *night*; curr 1988-1992] daylights

> **1988** It scares me out of the daynights. {Erin Huth, conv, Mar}

eggnod *n* [Tim Huth's word; < mispron of *eggnog*; curr ca 1992-] eggnog

> **1996** "Good news, kids—we got…eggnod." "Yey!" {Geof, then Erin & Tim Huth together, conv, 17 Nov}

furp *vt* [Erin Huth's word; < derived from a story where Geof Huth flipped the rearview mirror in this manner, while calling Erin a "Furp," her word for the

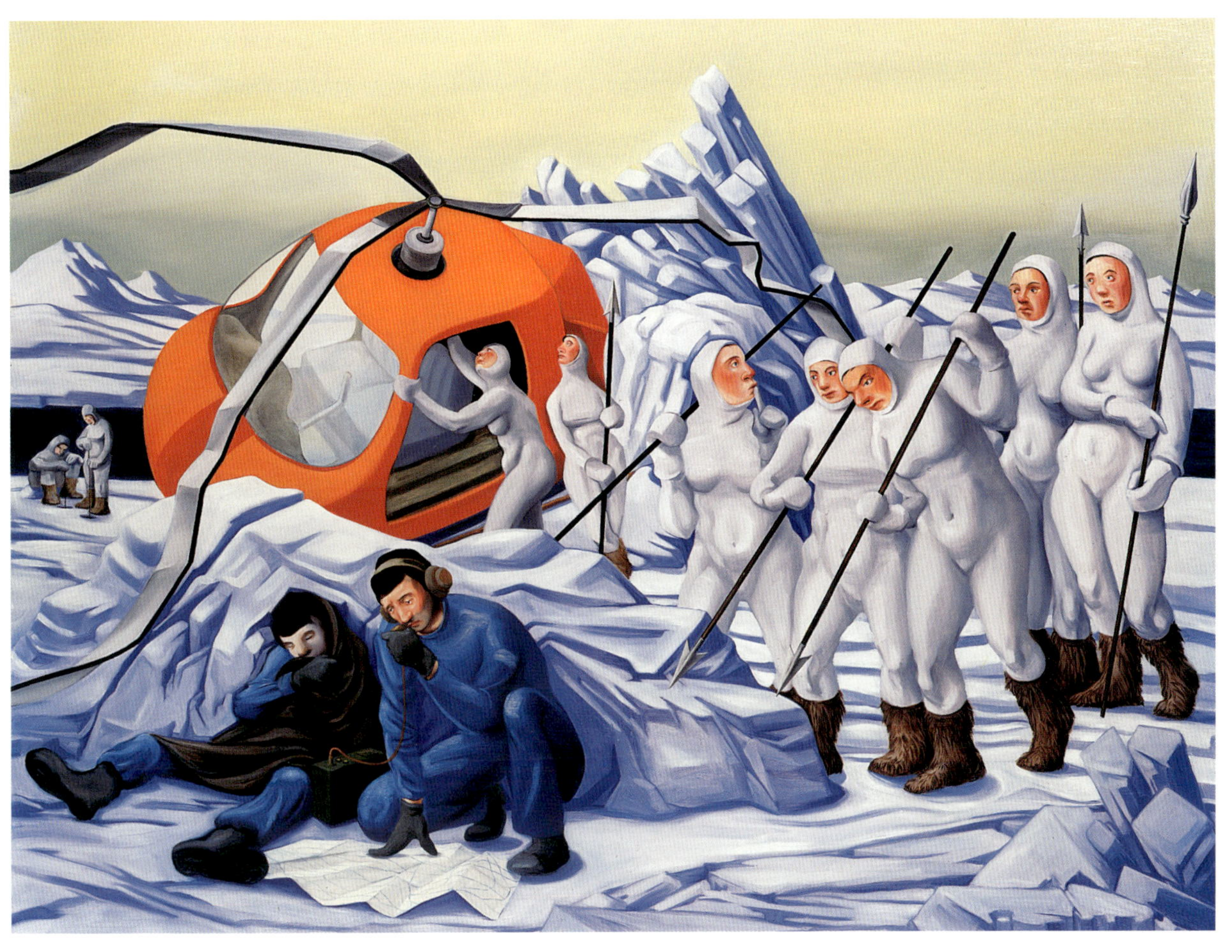

Geof Huth
Microglossary of Huthian Family Words, based on
Familiar Words: How
We Speak Alone Together, 1996

Book
Courtesy of the artist

Nicole Eisenman
Hunting, 2000

Oil on wood panel
43 x 56
Collection of Mr. and Mrs. Daniel M. Holtz, Miami, Fl
Courtesy of the artist and Tilton/Kustera
Gallery, New York

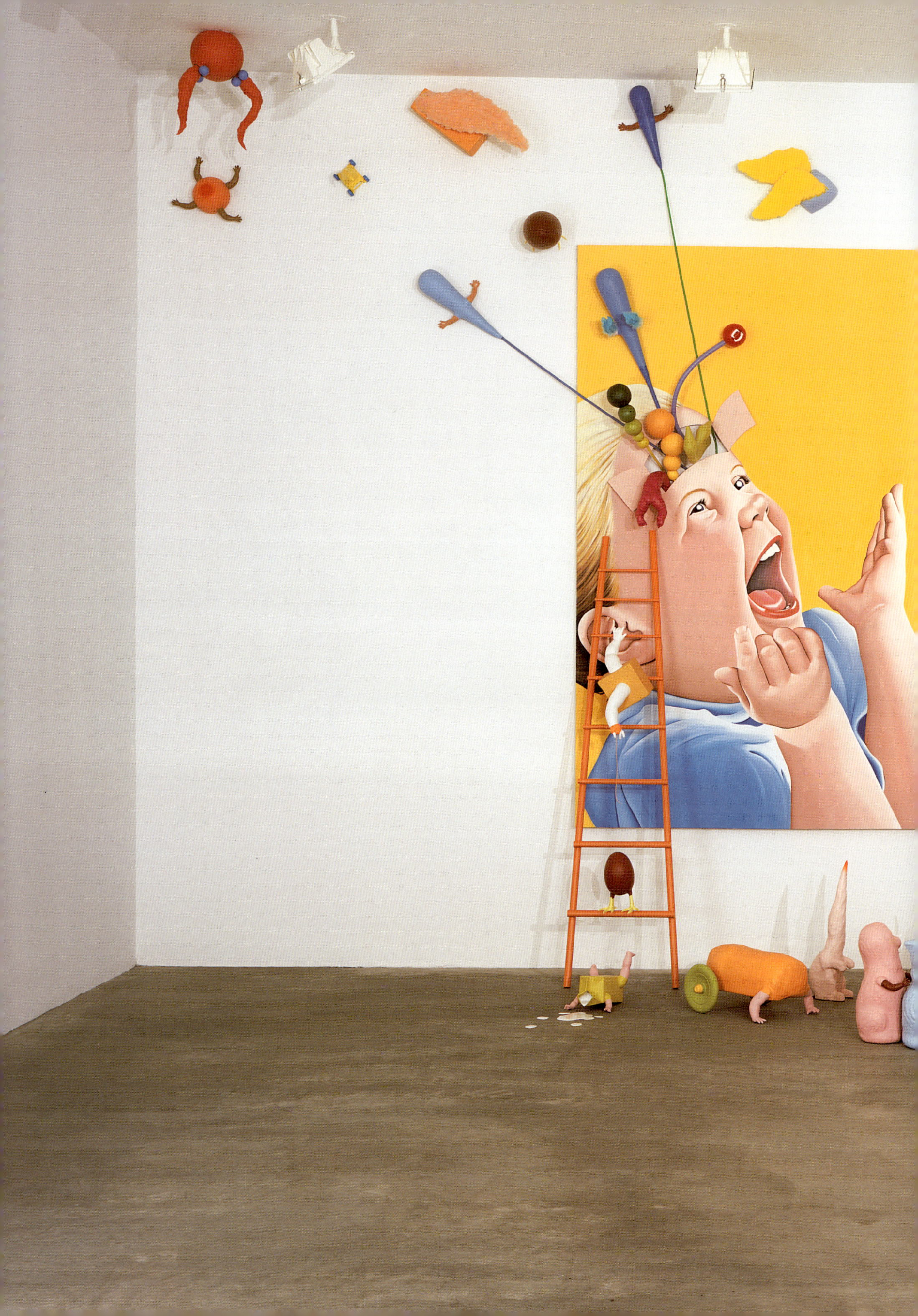

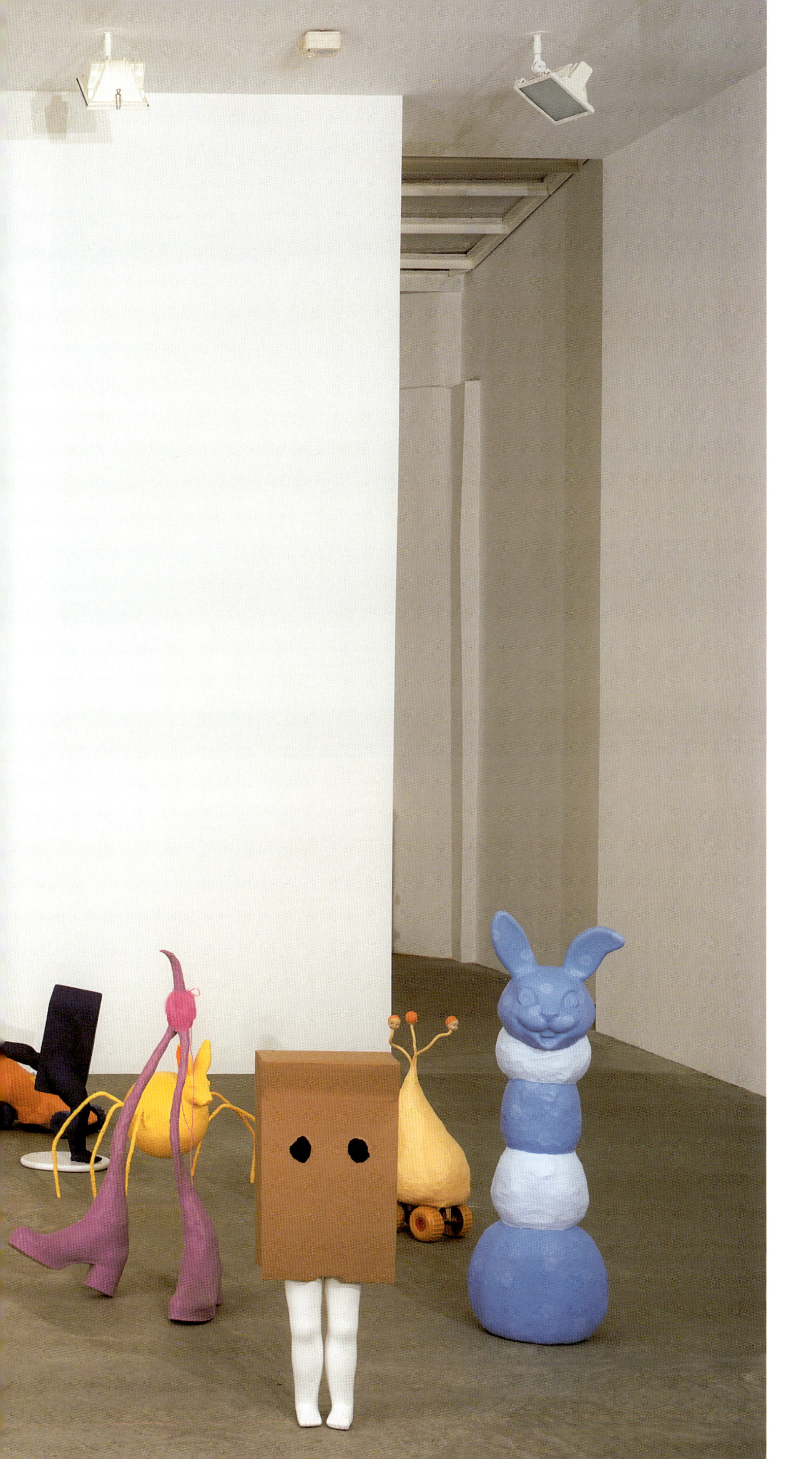

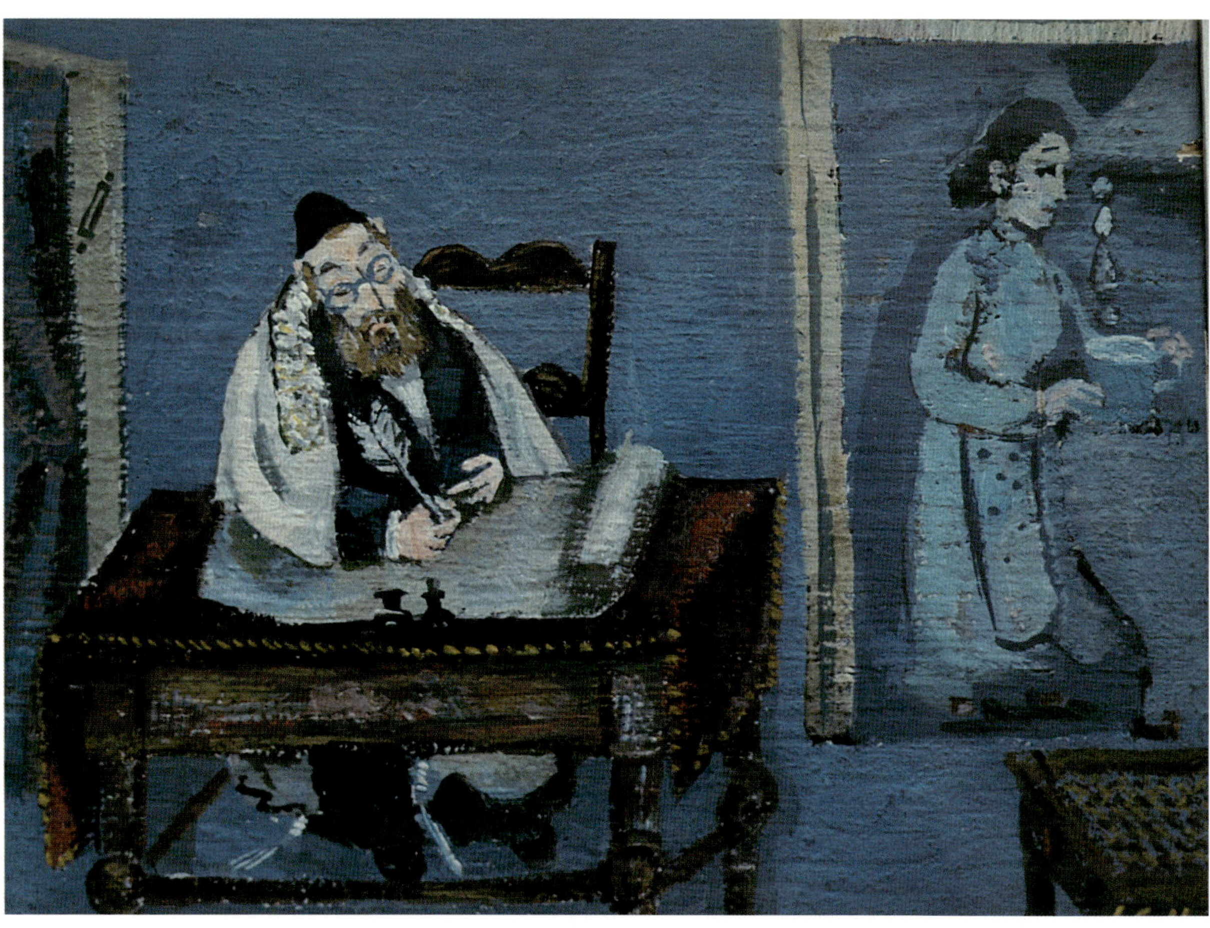

Sean Mellyn
It's a Beautiful Day, 2000

Oil on canvas, mixed media (29 objects)
Canvas size 96 x 60; overall dimensions variable
Courtesy Tilton/Kustera Gallery, New York

Mira Schor with Ilya Schor
Modest (detail showing 2 of 3 components), mid-1950s-2000
Painting installation including:

> **Mira Schor**
> *Modest Painting*, 2000
> Ink and gesso on linen; 12 x 6

> **Ilya Schor**
> *Scribe at Home*, mid-1950s
> Gouache on plywood; image size approx. 7 3/4 x 9 3/4

> **Mira Schor**
> *Modest Painting*, 2000
> Ink and gesso on linen; 12 x 6

Courtesy Mira Schor and the estate of Ilya Schor

I'd like to
put forward
the notion of
modest painting

Marriage

My husband likes to watch the cooking shows, the building shows,
the Discovery Channel, and the surgery channel.
Last night, he told us about a man who came into the emergency room

with a bayonet stuck entirely through his skull and brain.
Did they get it out? we all asked.
They did. And the man was O.K. because the blade went exactly between

the two halves without severing them.
And who had shoved this bayonet into the man's head? His wife.
A strong woman, someone said. And everyone else agreed.

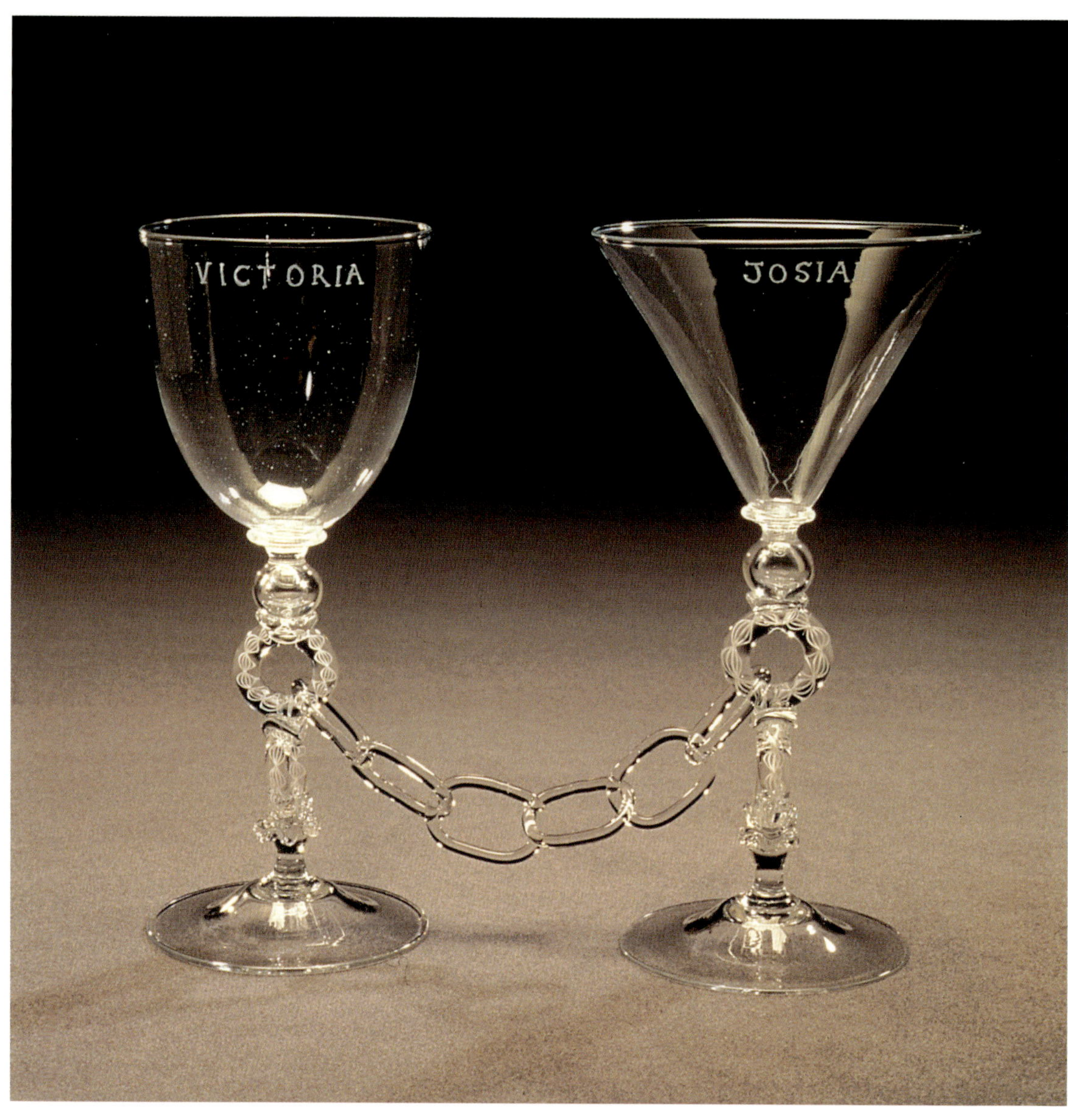

Josiah McElheny
Pledge: The First Glass Loving
Cups [Replica] Commission, 1994

Blown glass, engraved, flameworked,
certificate, display case
Glass object 8 x 8 x 3
Courtesy of the artist and
Donald Young Gallery, Chicago

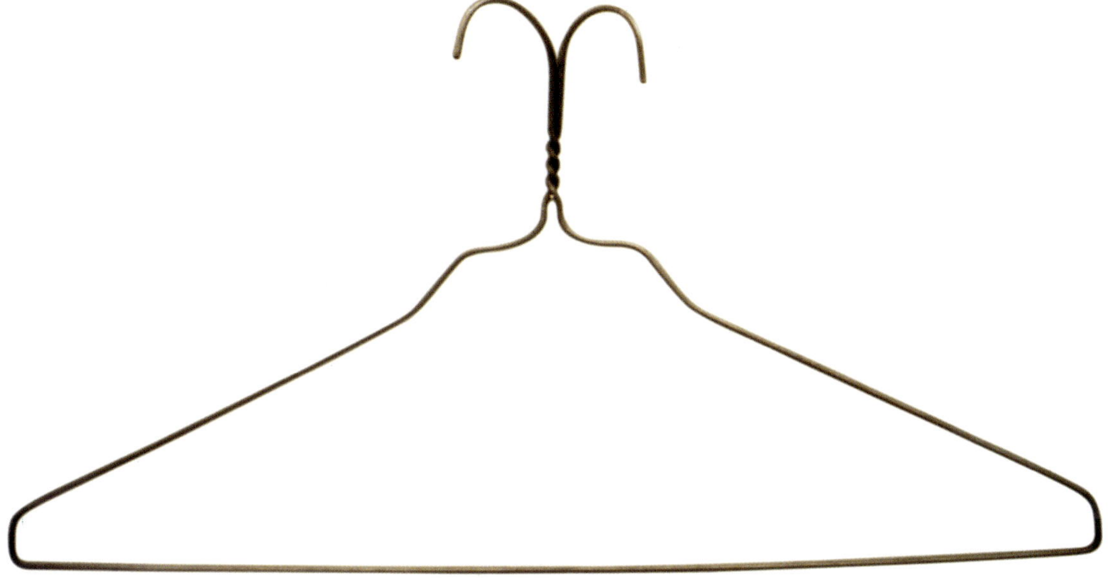

Ginger Krebs
Conjoined Hanger, 1997

Steel
9 x 16 x 1 1/2
Collection of Pat Goizetti
and Theresa Quinn, Chicago
Courtesy of the artist

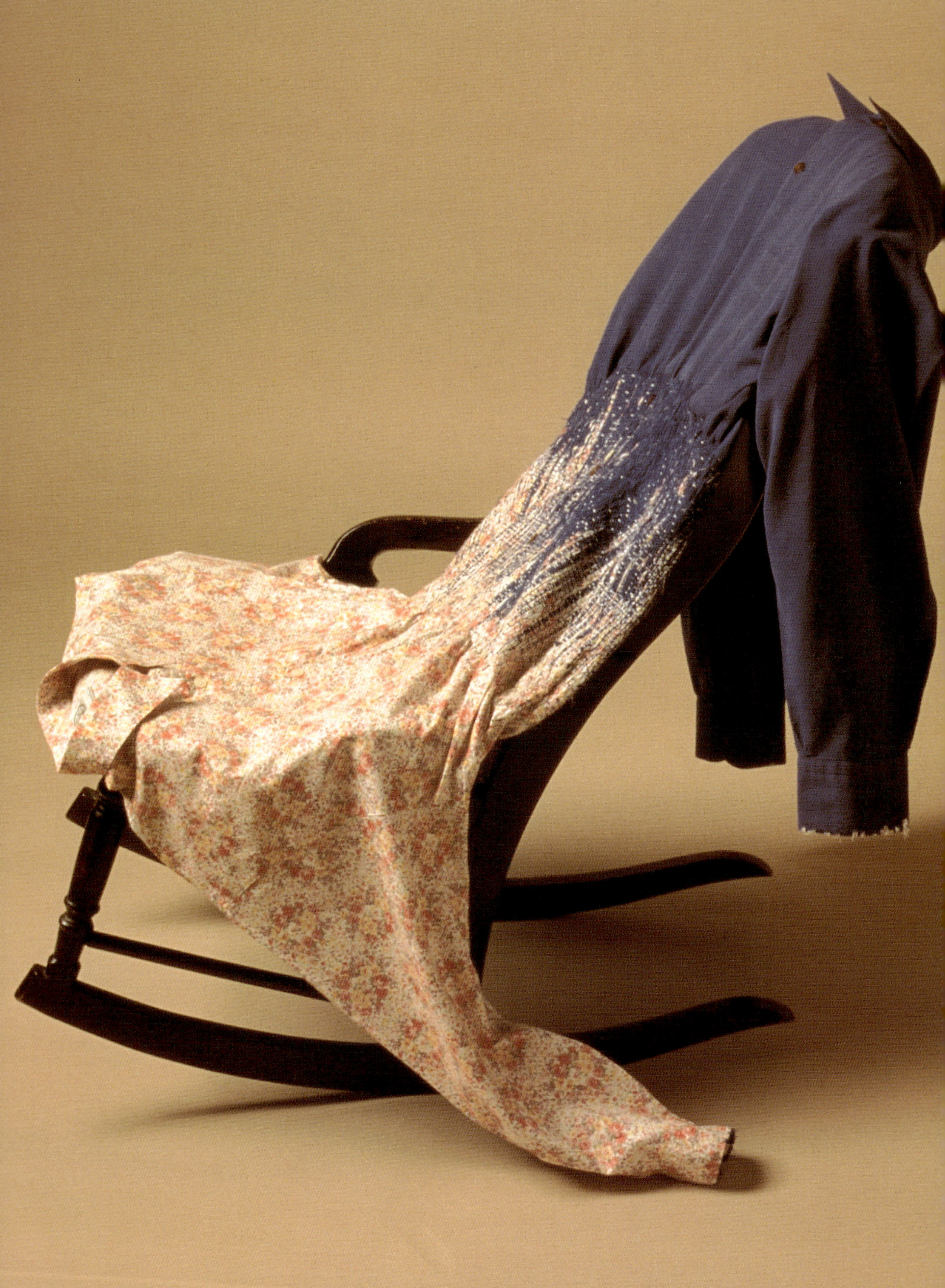

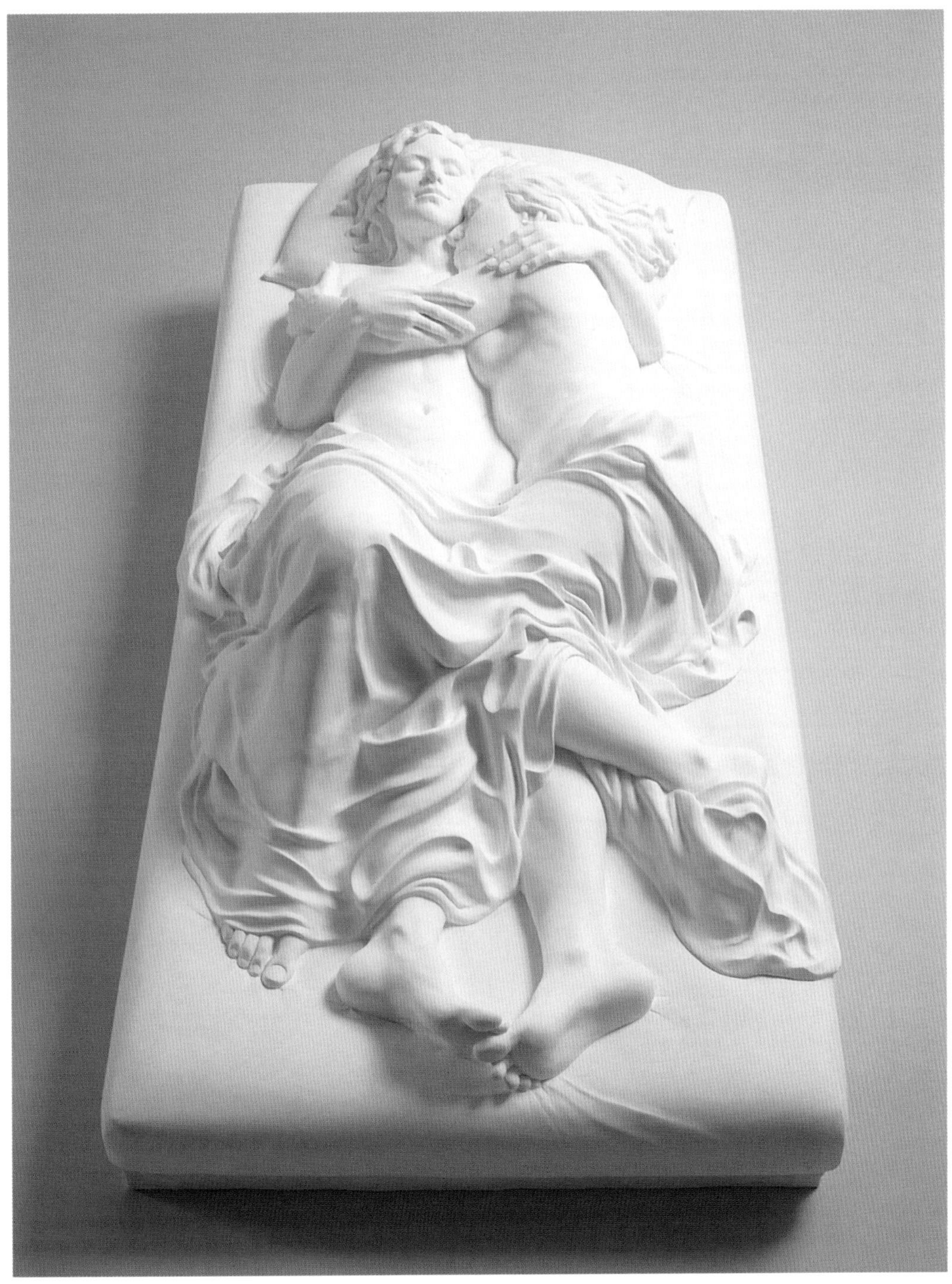

Ginger Krebs
Untitled, 1999

Secondhand shirts, cotton warp
63 x 48 x 2
Courtesy of the artist

Patricia Cronin
Memorial to a Marriage, 2001-02

Cast and carved plaster
17 x 27 x 53
Courtesy of the artist

His Costume

Somehow I never stopped to notice
that my father liked to dress as a woman.
He had his sign language about women
talking too much, and being stupid,
but whenever there was a costume party
he would dress like us, the tennis balls
for breasts—balls for breasts—the long
blond wig, the lipstick, he would sway
his body with moves of gracefulness
as if one being could be the whole
universe, its ends curving back to come
up from behind it. Six feet, and maybe
one-eighty, one-ninety, he had the shapely
legs of a male Grable—in a short
skirt, he leaned against a bookcase pillar
nursing his fifth drink, gazing
around from inside his mascara purdah
with those salty eyes. The woman from next door
had a tail and ears, she was covered in Reynolds Wrap,
she was Kitty Foyle, and my mother was in
a tiny tuxedo, but he always won
the prize. Those nights, he had a look of daring,
a look of triumph, of having stolen
back. And as far as I knew, he never threw
up, as a woman, or passed out, or made
those signals of scorn with his hands, just leaned,
voluptuous, at ease, deeply
present, as if sensing his full potential, crossing
over into himself, and back,
over, and back.

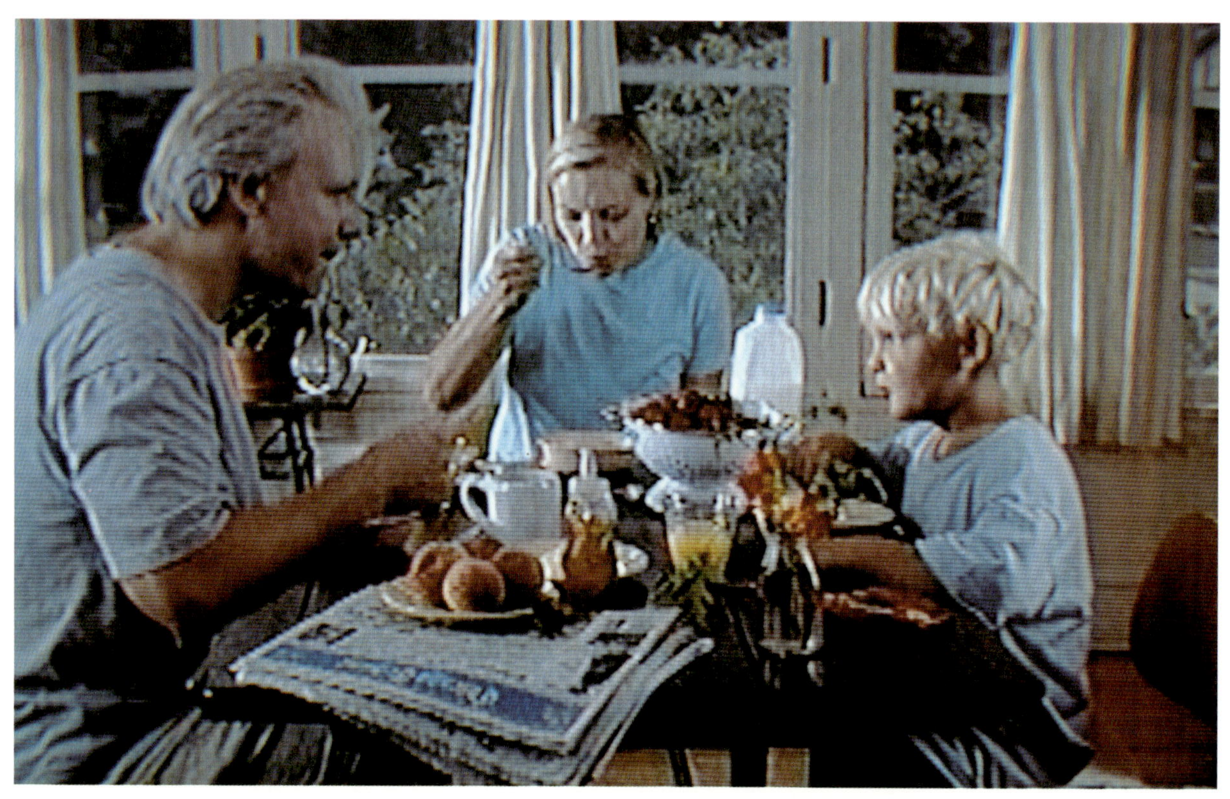

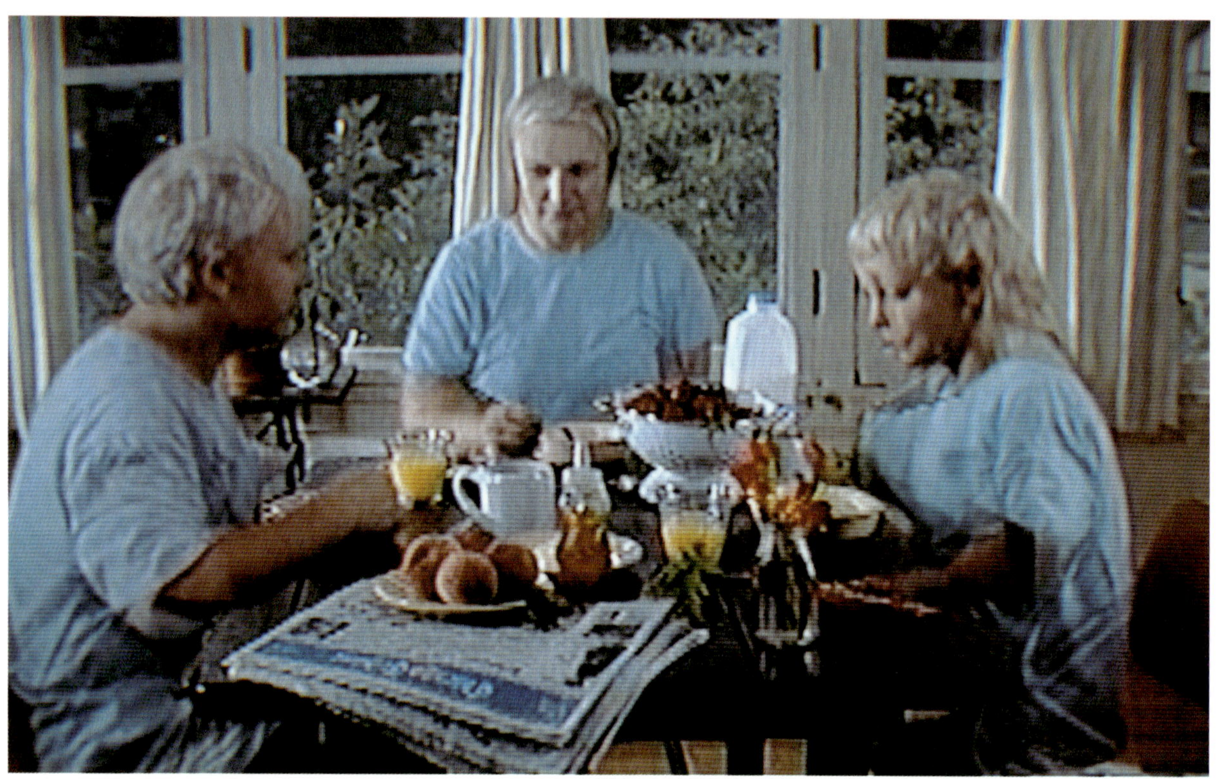

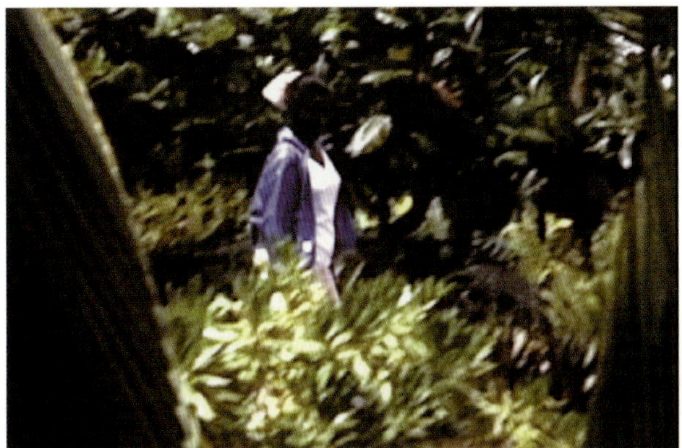

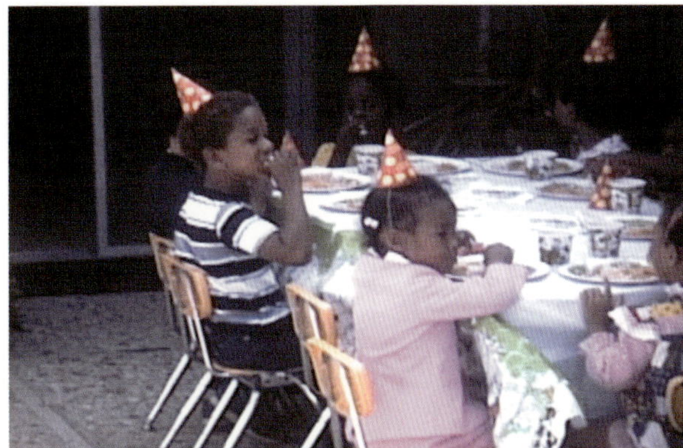

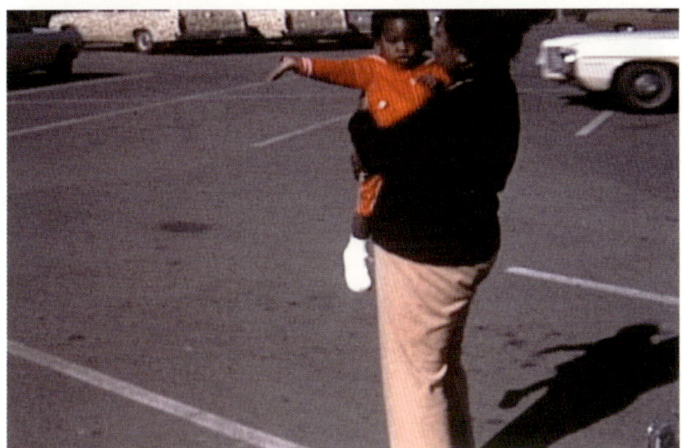

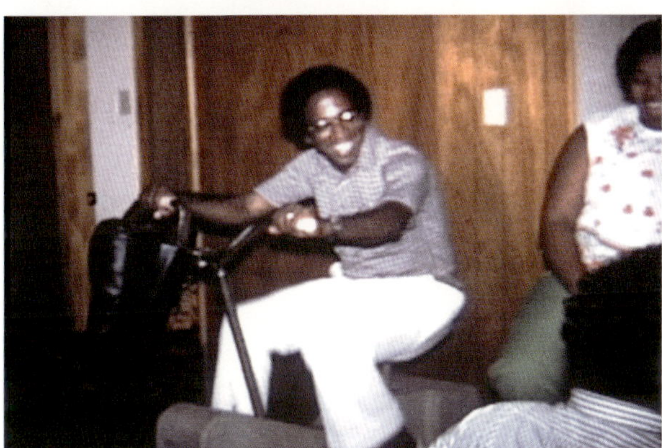

Preceding Page

Tony Tasset
I AM U R ME (video stills), 1998

Video transferred to DVD; color, sound;
30 second loop
Courtesy Feigen Contemporary, New York

Sanford Biggers
Racine de Mémoire (video stills), 2002

Salvaged wood, mixed media, video projection;
Super 8 film converted to DVD, sound, color
Courtesy of the artist

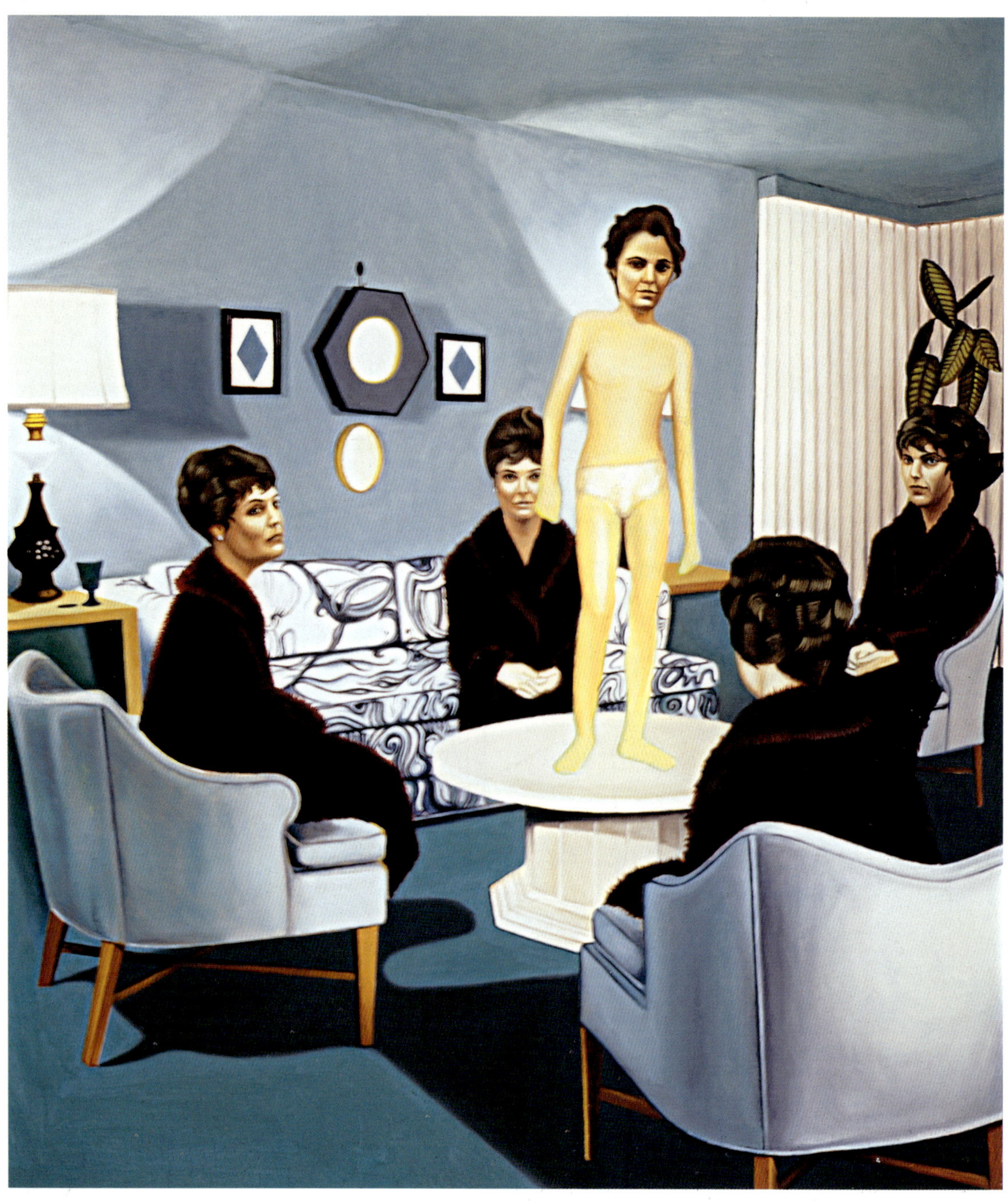

Sandra Scolnik
The Sisters, 1998-99

Oil on wood panel
10 x 8 1/2
Collection of Dominique Levy, New York
Courtesy CRG Gallery, New York

Following Page
Robert Melee
Me and Mommy, 2001

Slip cover, gilded frame, black and white,
and color photographs
65 1/2 x 53
Courtesy Andrew Kreps Gallery, New York

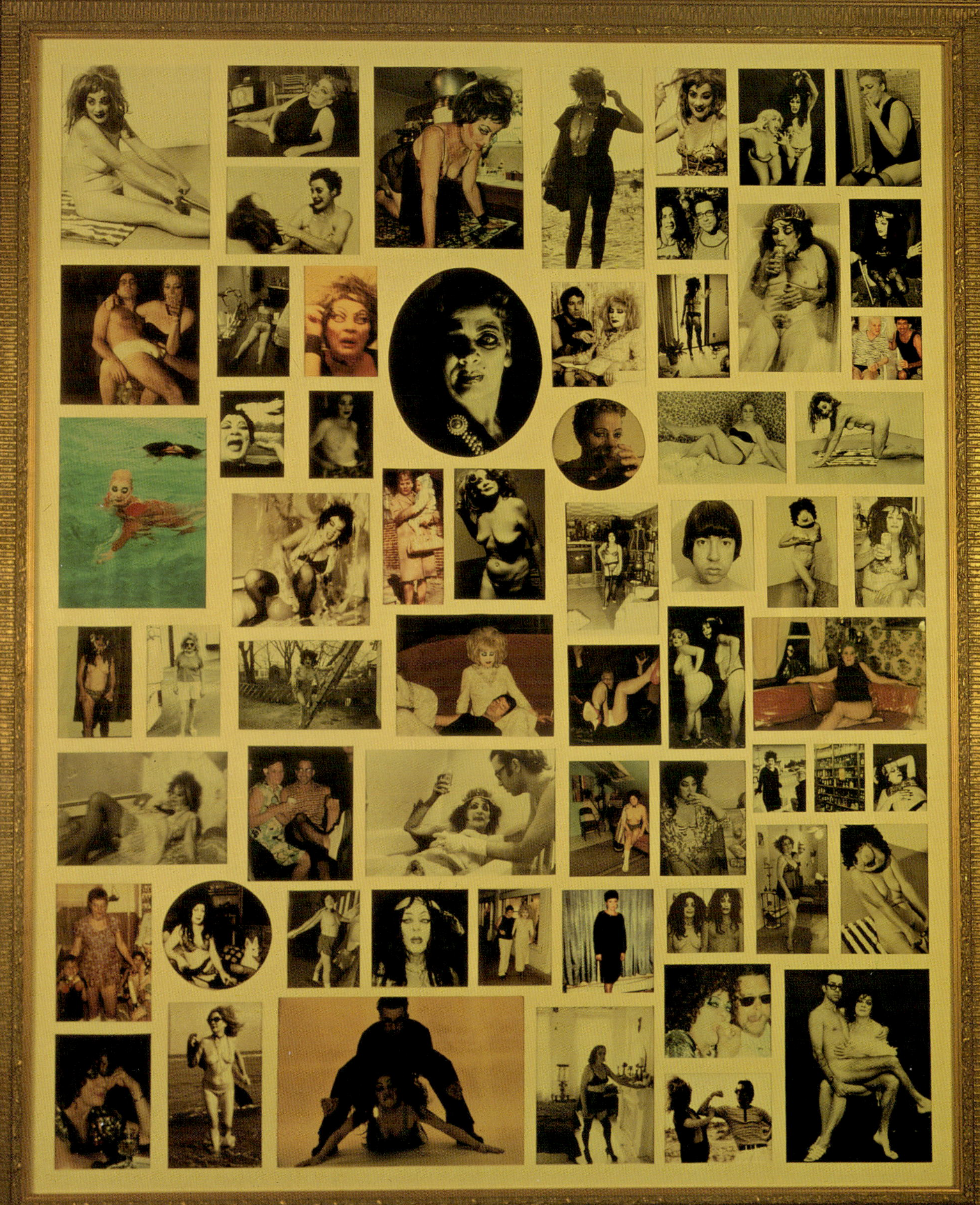

Linda Gregerson

A History Play

Months later—I'd been cleaning
        my desk—
    these bits of gold foil spilled to the ground

a second time, five-petalled blossoms of public
        gaud
    unloosed from the folded playbill as in

August from the heavens at the Swan, Act
        Five,
    to mark the child Elizabeth's birth.

The old queen has been put aside *(I am not
        such a truant as not
    to know)*, the new one's doomed *(the language

I have lived in)*, the girlchild is herself
        a sign of grace
    withheld. But look at these sumptuous

velvets with their branchwork and encrusted
        pearl,
    you'd think the hand of death would be afraid

to strike. That's wrong. You'd think
        that death
    had held the needle and dispensed the worm-

wrought thread. The players will be wanting their late
        supper soon, while
    we–we two and our two girls–

set out across the footbridge on our way back
        home.
    The waterfowl will be asleep–they're sleeping

already—their willow-strewn and fecal
        island silent
    in the summer night. The past that for a moment

turned, backlit, thick
        with presence, as though
    leading to us somehow, in its very

inadvertance giving way to this
            slight stench
      beneath a moon-washed bridge, the past

that has a place for us will know us by
            our scattered
      wake. *(A strange tongue makes)* And morning

meanwhile yet to come *(my cause
            more strange):*
      the girls will have hot chocolate with their toast

and eggs. The play? (which we will talk about) Tenacious
            in its
      praise and fierce in its elisions. So

father, mother (older than the cast-off queen), two
            girls: an open book.
      And spilling from the binding, gold.

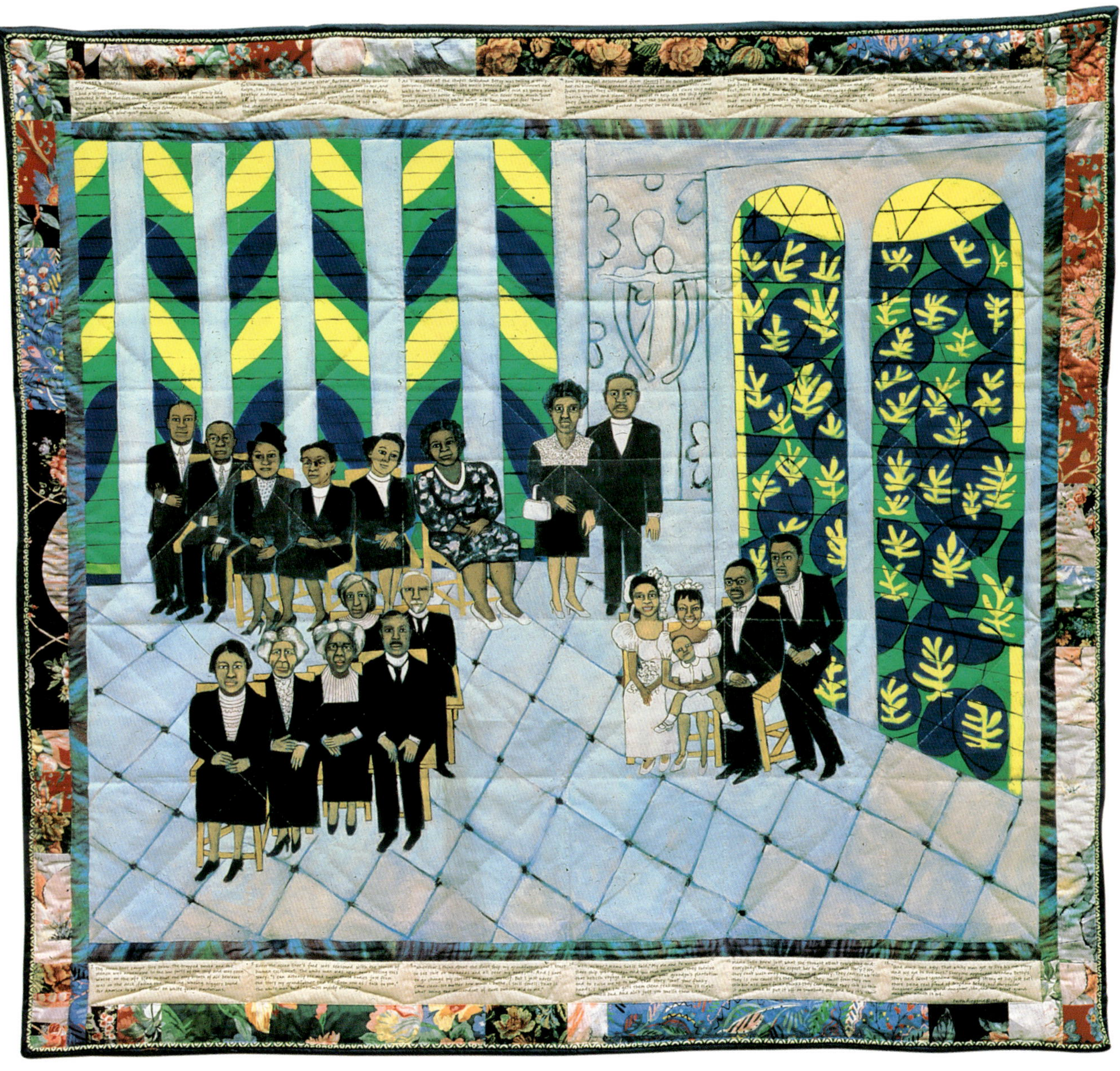

Faith Ringgold

Matisse's Chapel (The French
Collection, Part 1, #6), 1991

Acrylic on canvas with fabric border
74 x 79 1/2
Collection of George and Joyce Wein, New York
Courtesy of the artist and ACA Galleries, New York

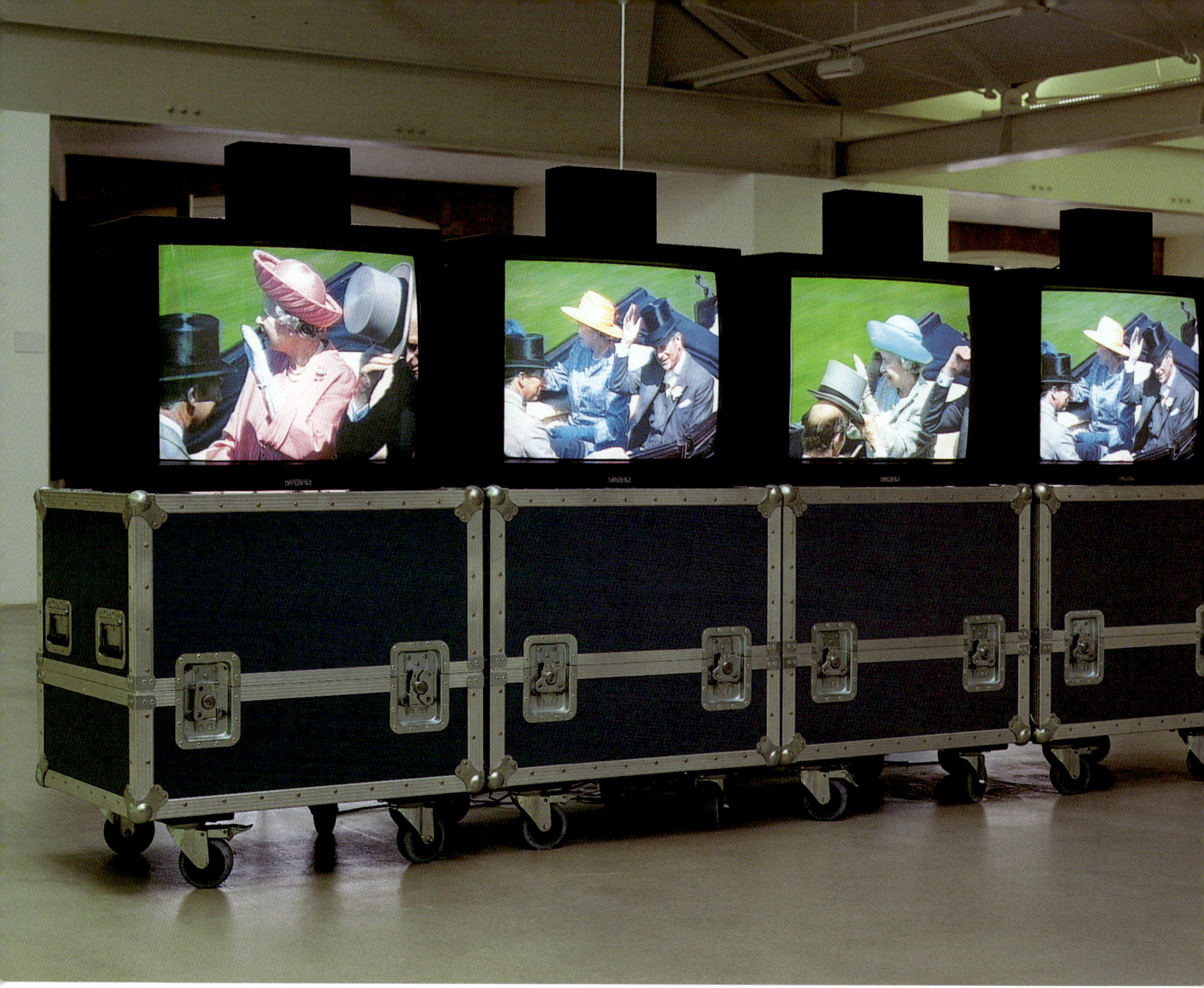

Mark Wallinger
Royal Ascot (installation view), 1994

Video installation consisting of 4 monitors,
4 DVD players, sync unit, 4 speakers, 4 flight
cases; edition of 3
Approx. 72 x 114 x 30 3/4
Collection of the British Council
Courtesy Anthony Reynolds Gallery, London

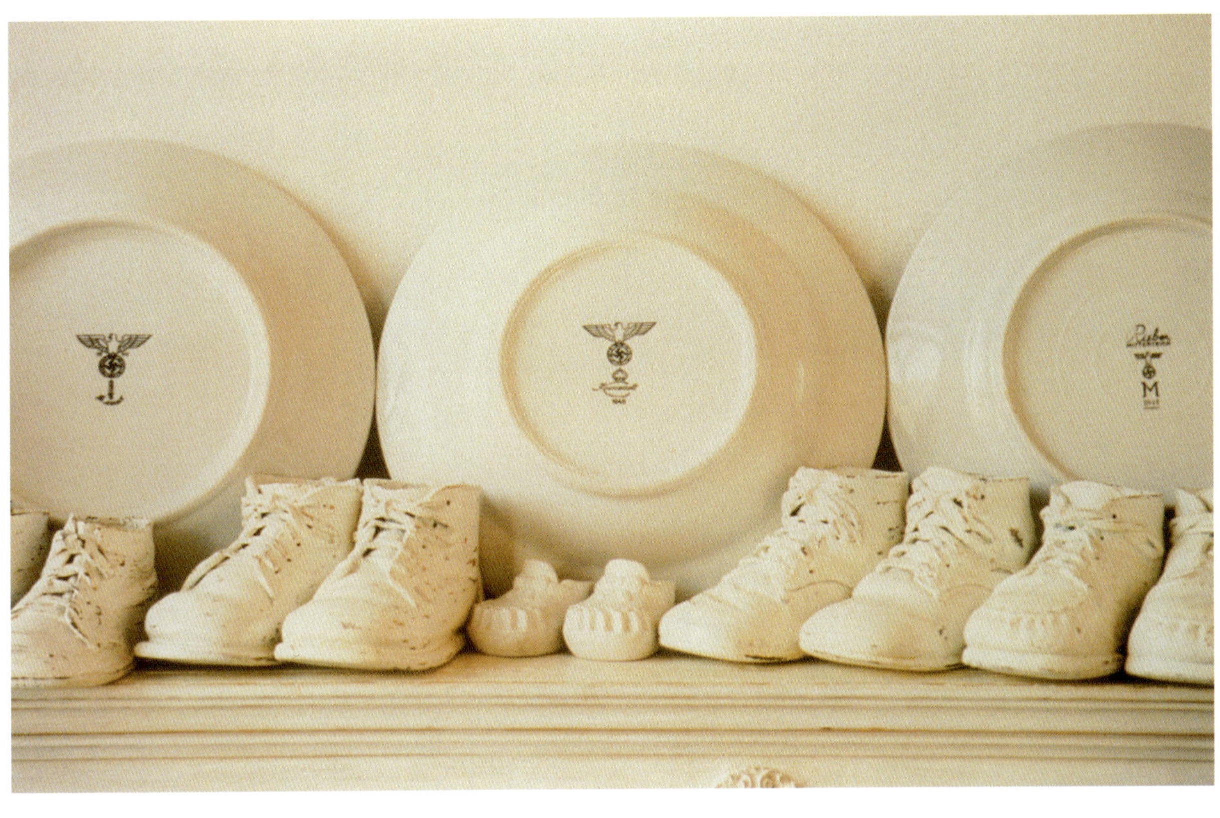

Ernesto Pujol
Still-life #3 (from the *Whiteness* series), 1998

C-print photograph
8 x 13 unframed
Courtesy of the artist and Galeria Ramis Barquet, New York

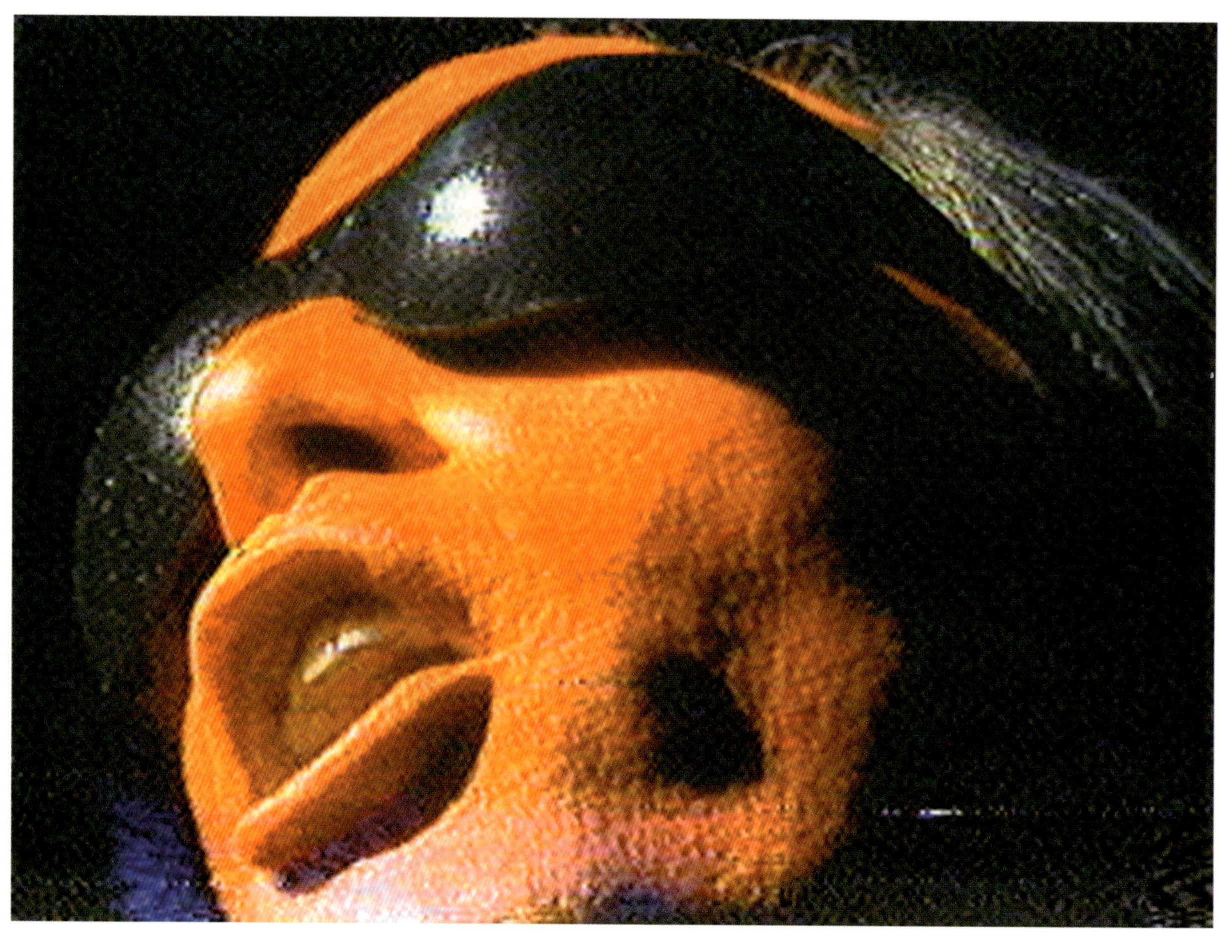

Doug Hall

These Are the Rules (video still), 1998

Video transferred to DVD; color, sound;
4:39 minutes
Courtesy of Electronic Arts Intermix, New York

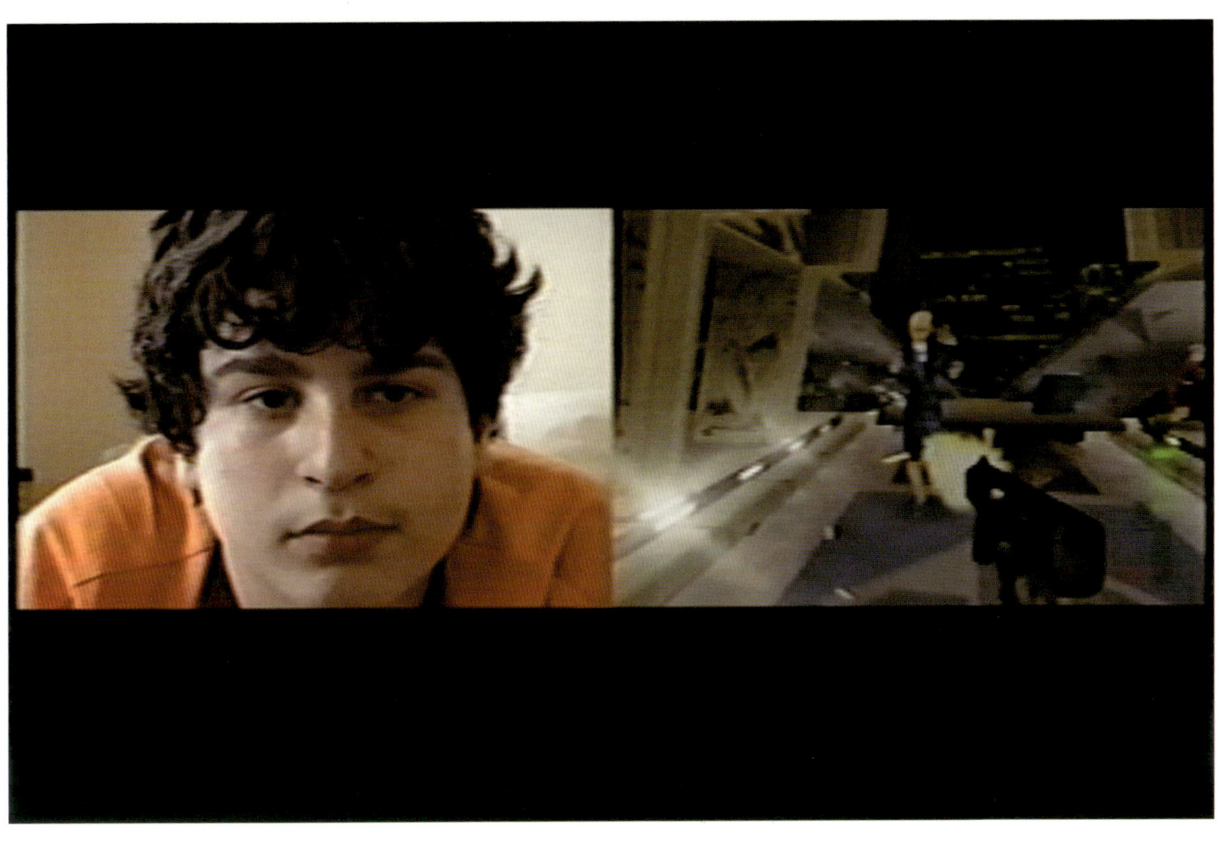

Barbara Pollack
Perfect Dark (video still), 2001

Video installation; color, sound; 4:30 minutes
Courtesy of the artist

Mother and Child

We're all dreamers; we don't know who we are.

Some machine made us; machine of the world, the constricting family.
Then back to the world, polished by soft whips.

We dream; we don't remember.

Machine of the family: dark fur, forests of the mother's body.
Machine of the mother: white city inside her.

And before that: earth and water.
Moss between rocks, pieces of leaves and grass.

And before, cells in a great darkness.
And before that, the veiled world.

This is why you were born: to silence me.
Cells of my mother and father, it is your turn
to be pivotal, to be the masterpiece.

I improvised; I never remembered.
Now it's your turn to be driven;
you're the one who demands to know:

Why do I suffer? Why am I ignorant?
Cells in a great darkness. Some machine made us;
it is your turn to address it, to go back asking
what am I for? What am I for?

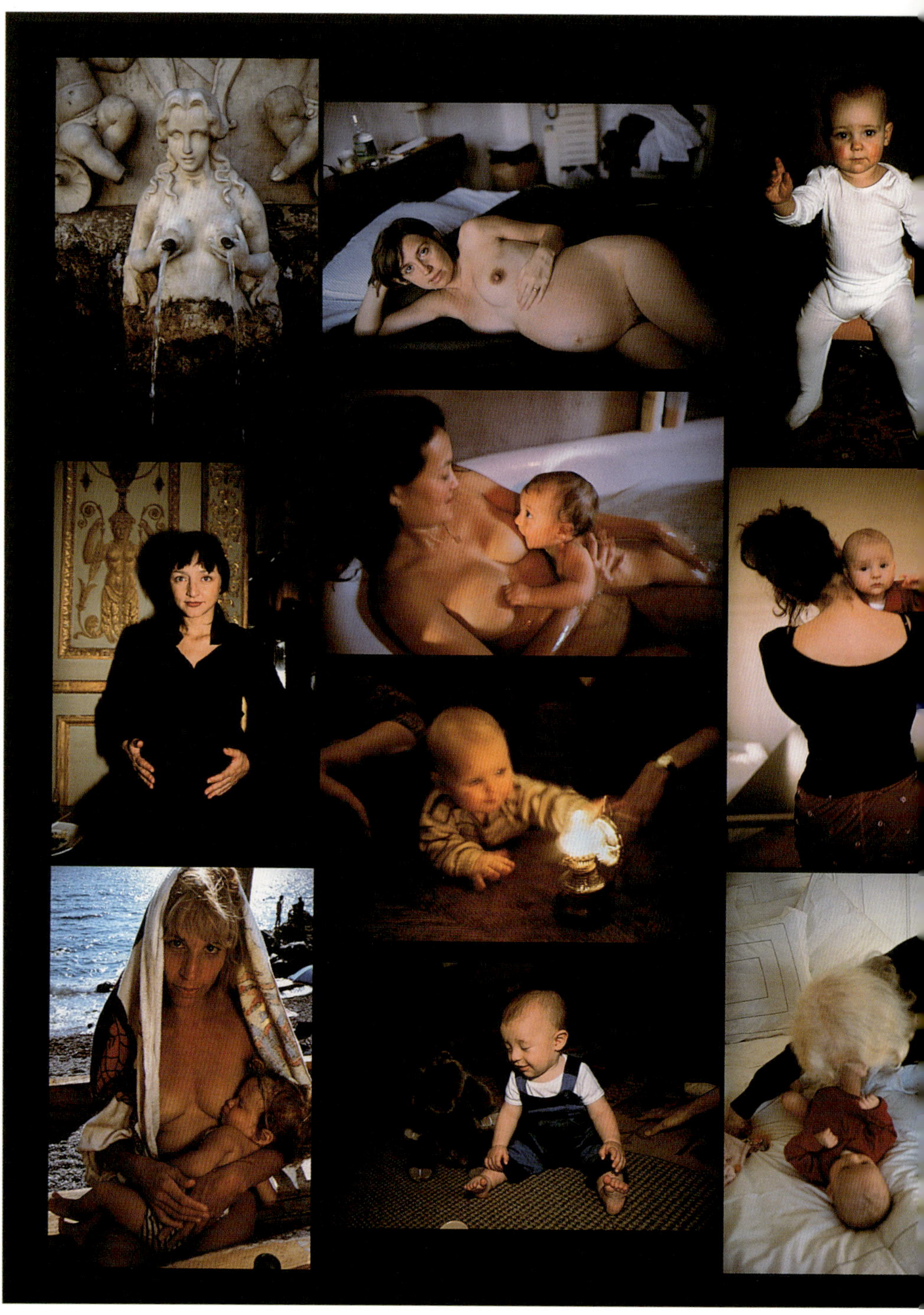

Nan Goldin

From Here to Maternity, 1986-2000/2000

24 mounted cibachrome prints
60 x 100
Courtesy of Matthew Marks Gallery, New York

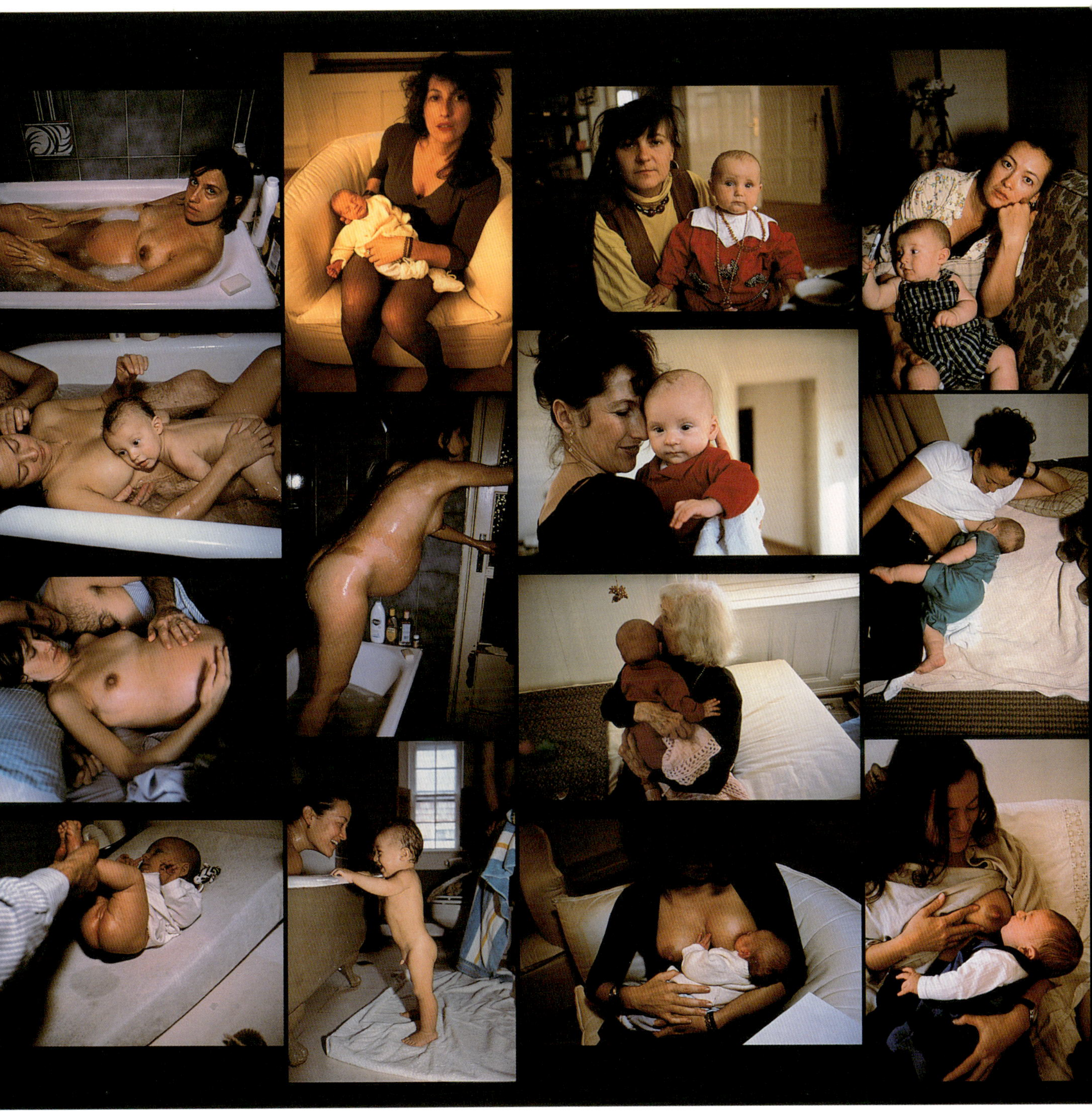

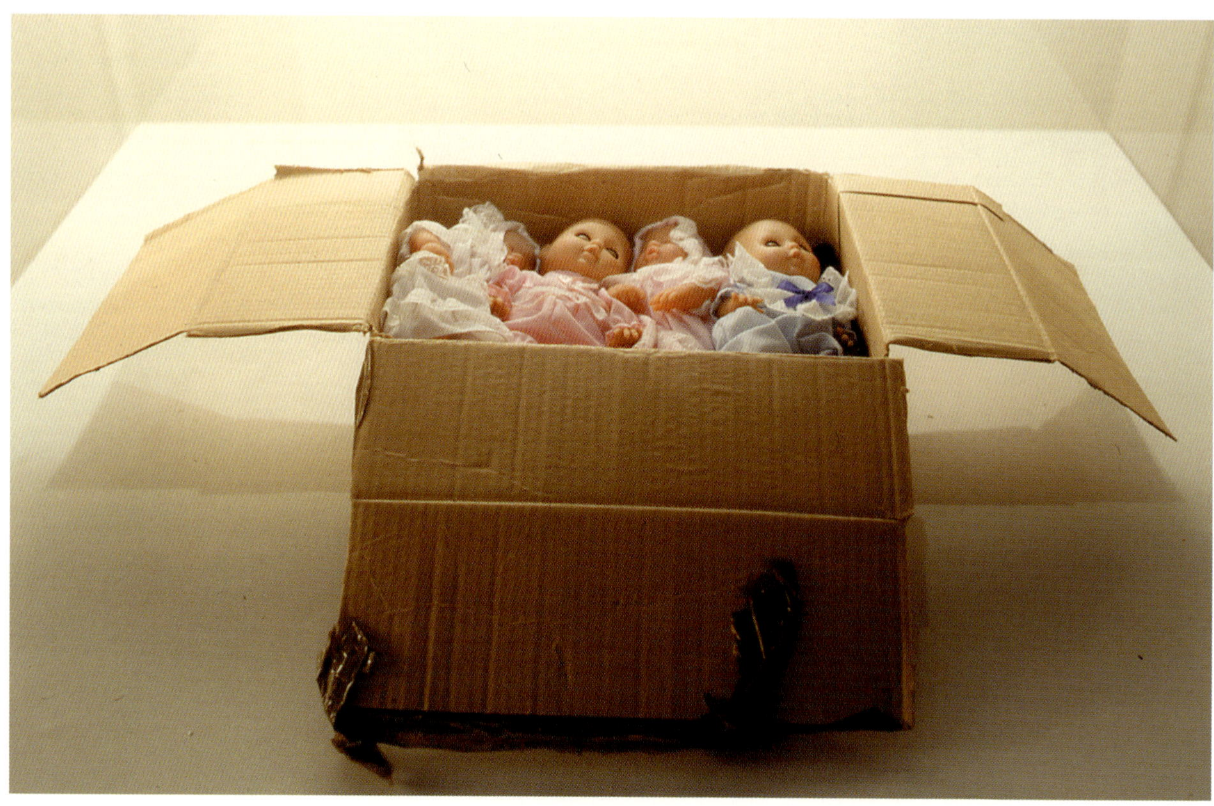

Olu Oguibe
Mementos, 1996

Mixed media with paper box, dolls, fabric
5 x 20 x 22 1/2
Collection of the artist

Following Pages
Jonathan Seliger
For a Family, 1995-96

Oil, alkyd, acrylic, modeling paste,
varnish, on canvas; lacquer on steel
44 1/2 x 19 x 19
Collection of the artist

Jin-me Yoon
Intersection V (installation view
at Catriona Jeffries Gallery), 2001

Framed C-prints
Diptych, 80 x 72 each
Courtesy of the artist and Catriona Jeffries
Gallery, Vancouver, British Columbia

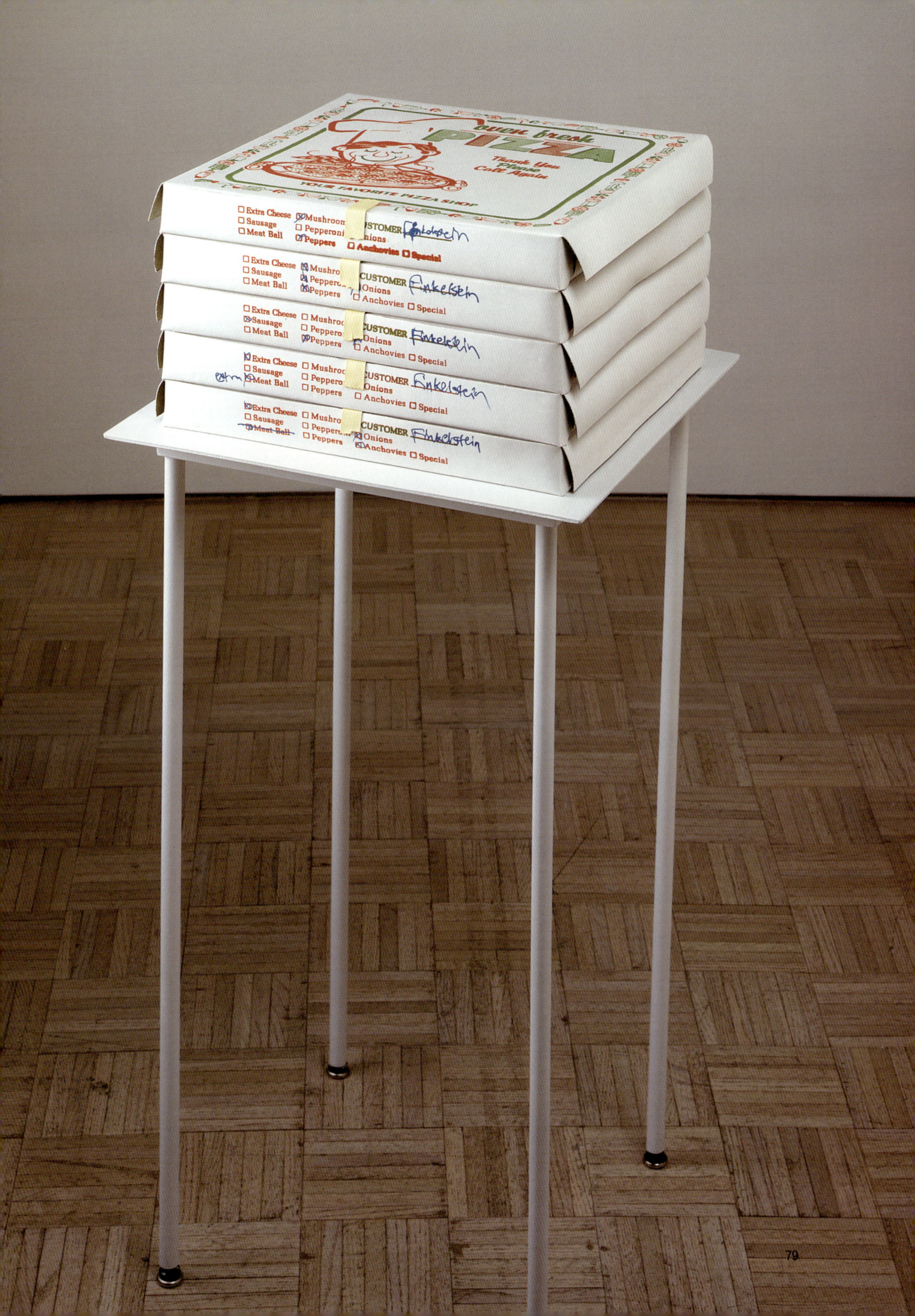
oven fresh
PIZZA
Thank You
Please
Call Again
YOUR FAVORITE PIZZA SHOP
Extra Cheese   Mushroom   CUSTOMER   Finkelstein
Sausage   Pepperoni   Onions
Meat Ball   Peppers   Anchovies   Special
Extra Cheese   Mushroom   CUSTOMER   Finkelstein
Sausage   Pepperoni   Onions
Meat Ball   Peppers   Anchovies   Special
Extra Cheese   Mushroom   CUSTOMER   Finkelstein
Sausage   Pepperoni   Onions
Meat Ball   Peppers   Anchovies   Special
Extra Cheese   Mushroom   CUSTOMER   Finkelstein
Sausage   Pepperoni   Onions
Meat Ball   Peppers   Anchovies   Special
Extra Cheese   Mushroom   CUSTOMER   Finkelstein
Sausage   Pepperoni   Onions
Meat Ball   Peppers   Anchovies   Special

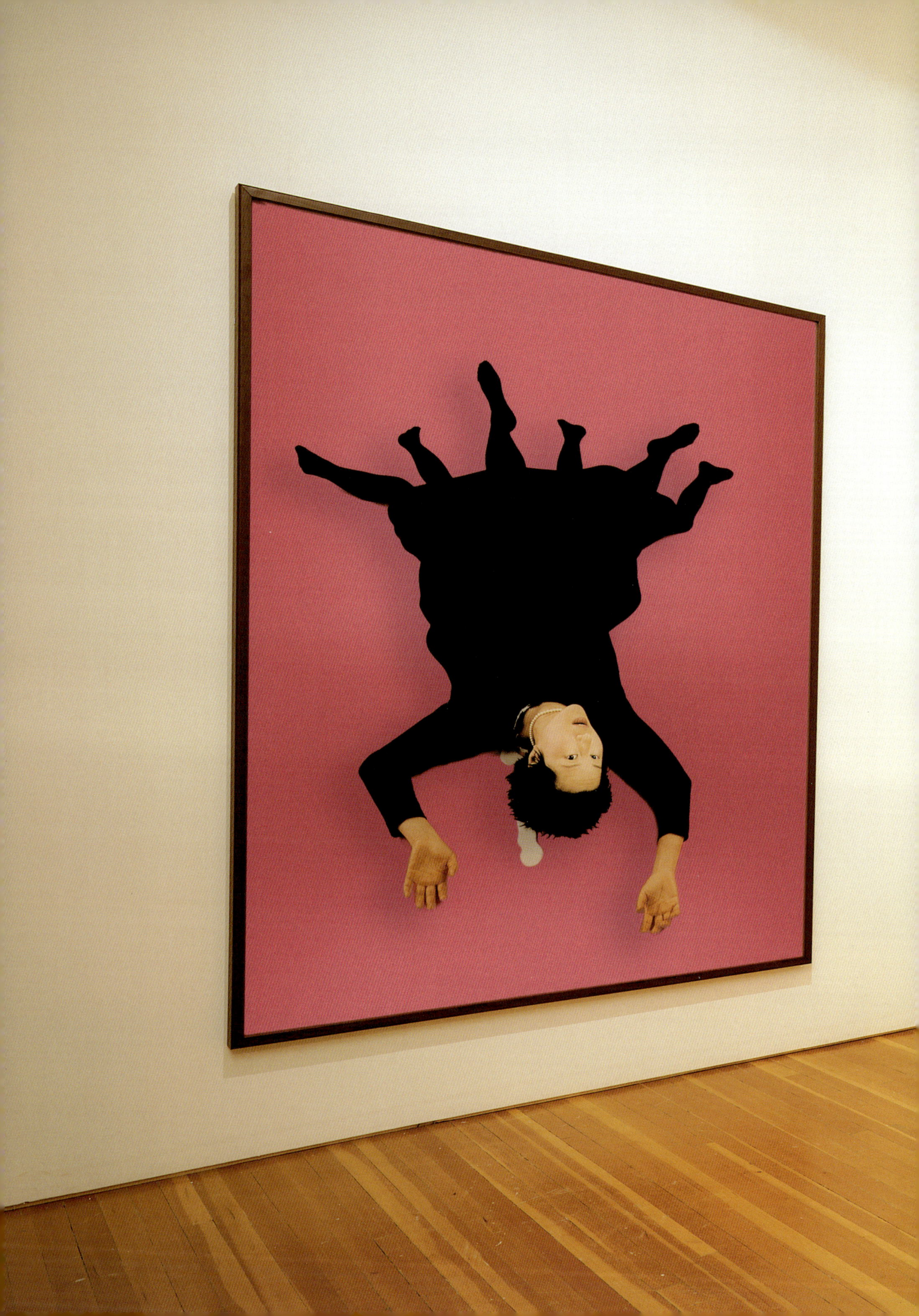

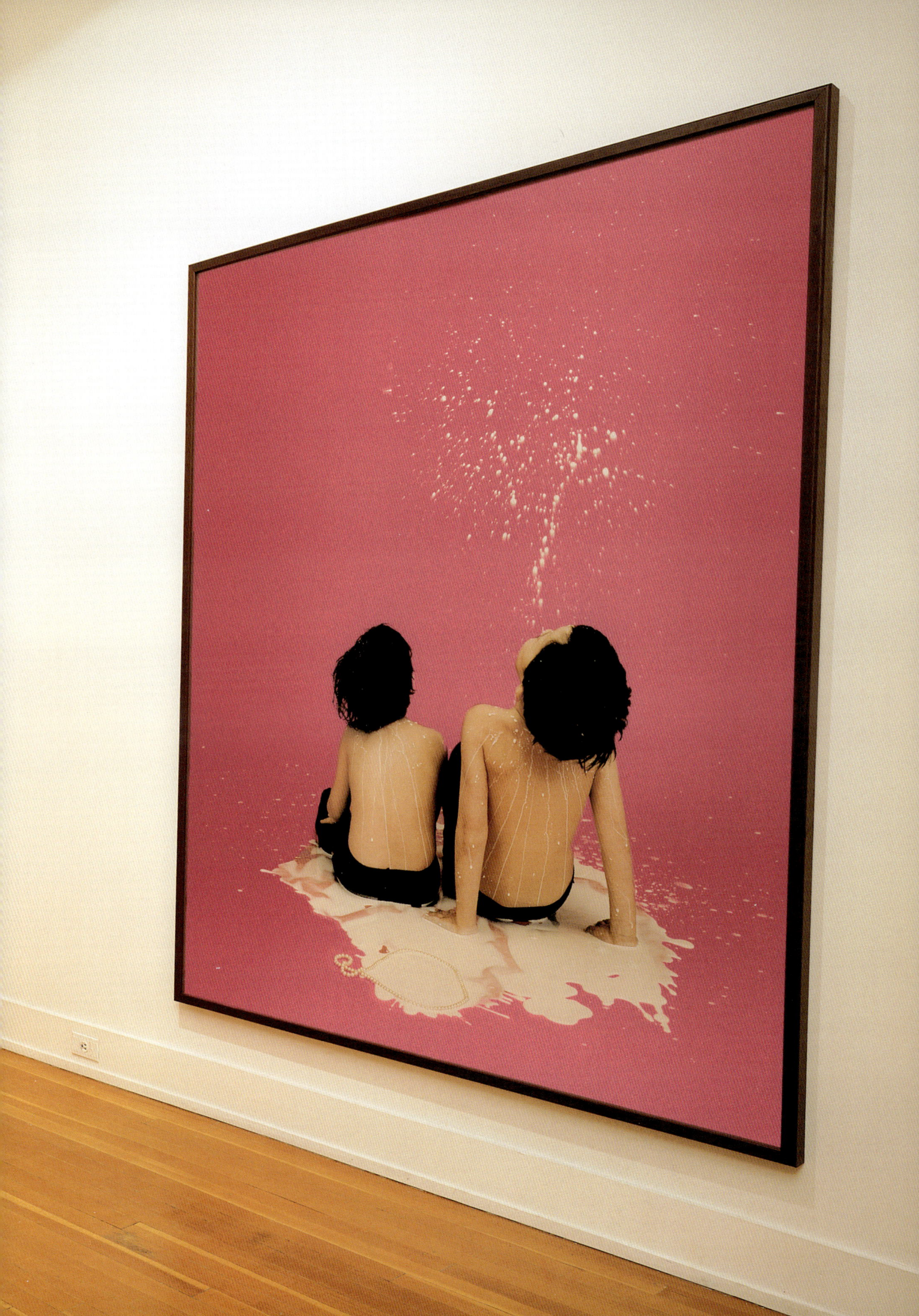

A Progression

I am wearing the last of the sheep.
Winter at the table devouring.
Father torpedoed by hail.
Mother forgetting his name.

I am wearing a necklace of caskets.
April at the table, my birthday.
Father napping, his wallet clutched.
The tip of Mother's nose, white frosting.

I wear a perennial garden.
July at the table perishes. Mother
wants to know who's that Southerner
over there, or is it a lion laughing?

I'm wearing their house around me.
September and the boiler full-blasting.
Father with an axe in the backyard, suspended.
Mother in the hallway, maybe.

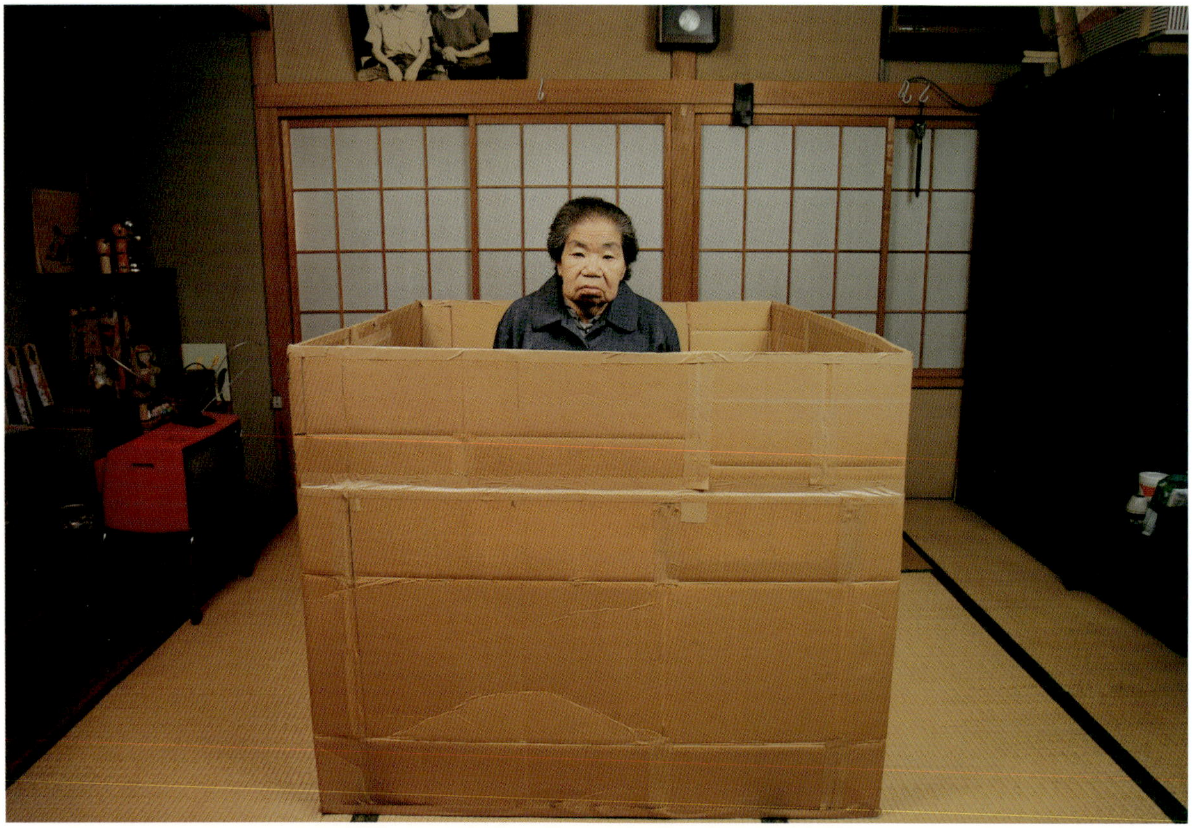

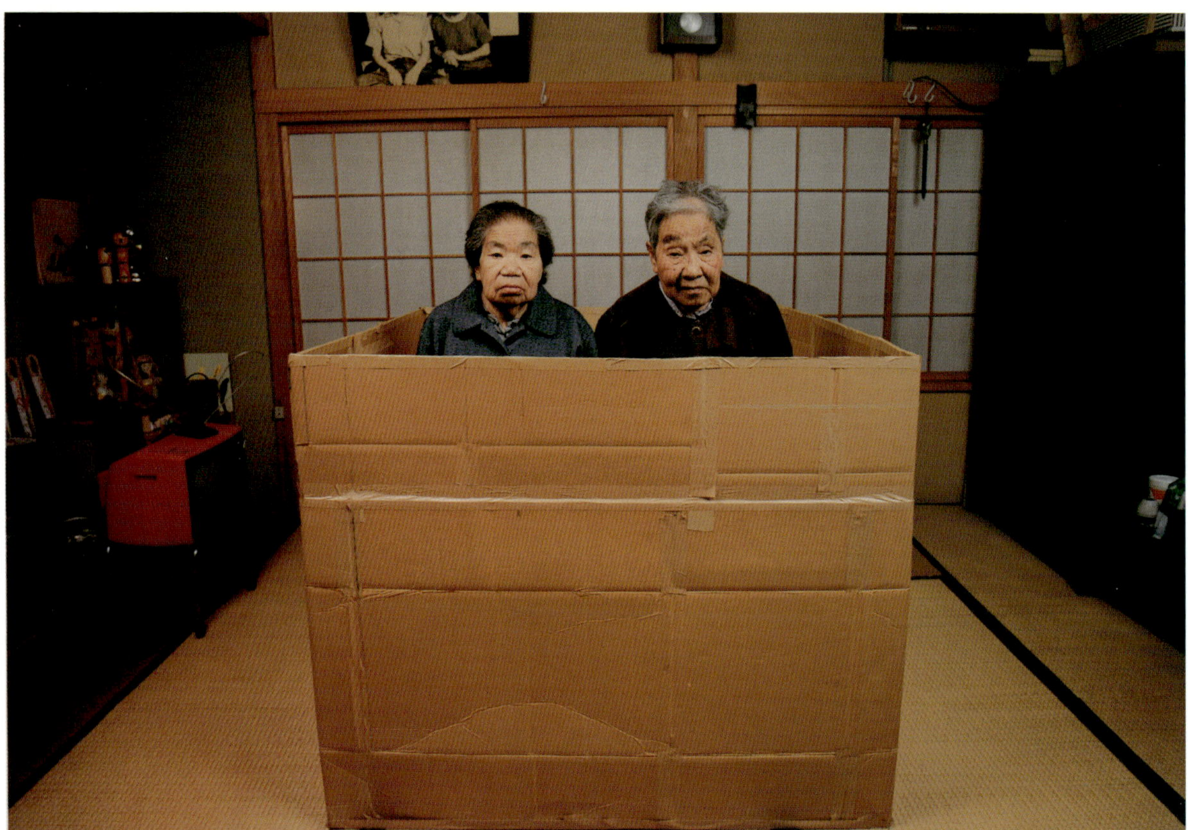

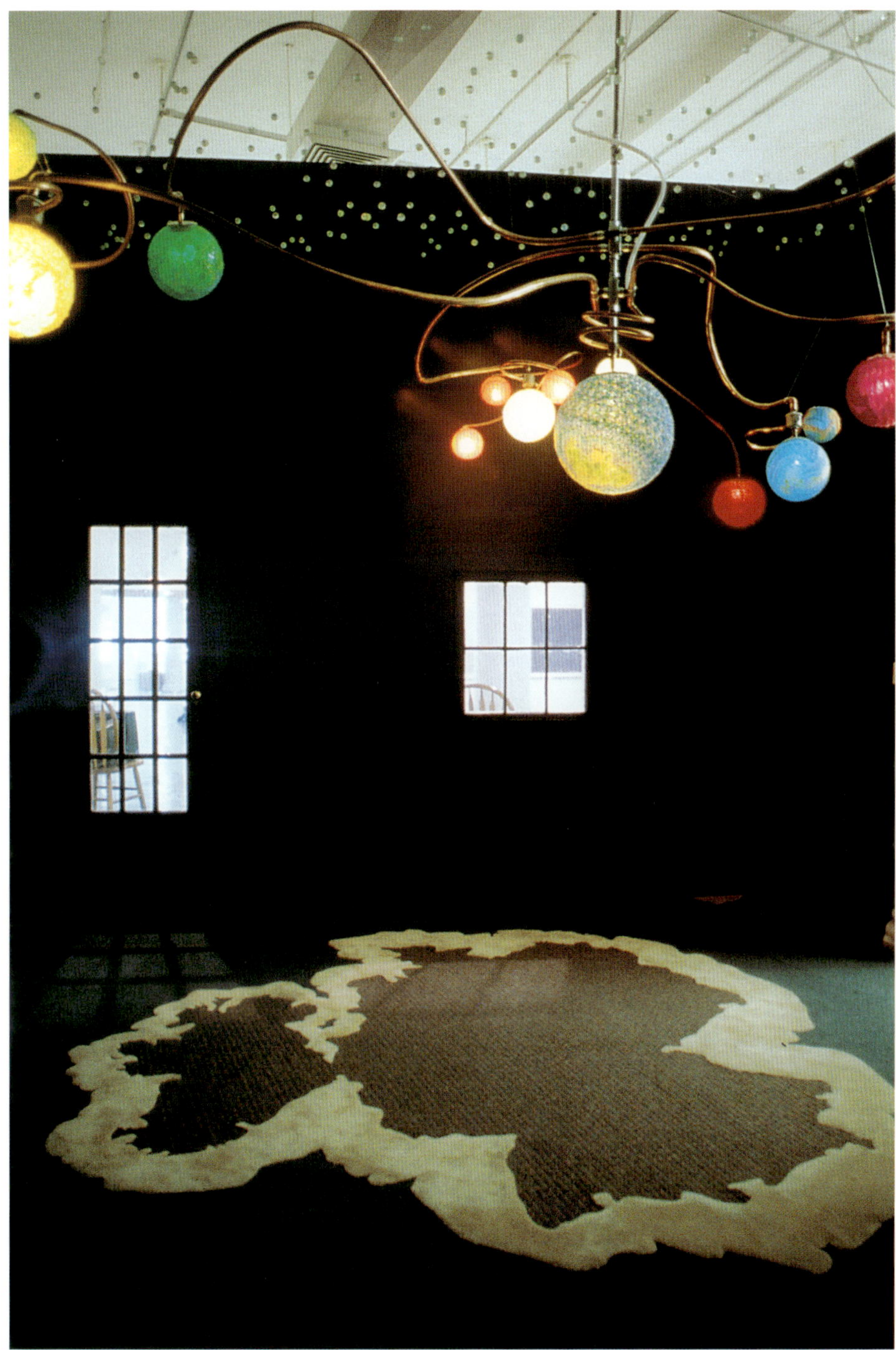

Tatsumi Orimoto
In the Box (Mama), 1997

Photograph
23 1/2 x 27 1/2

In the Box (Mama and Neighbor), 1997

Photograph
23 1/2 x 27 1/2
Courtesy of the artist

John Corbin
1000 Plateaus: Alliances and

Liaisons (installation view at
The New Museum of Contemporary Art,
New York), 1998/2002

Acrylic globes, copper tubing, polymer emulsion,
carpeting, light bulbs, housed in wooden construction
Dimensions variable
Courtesy of the artist

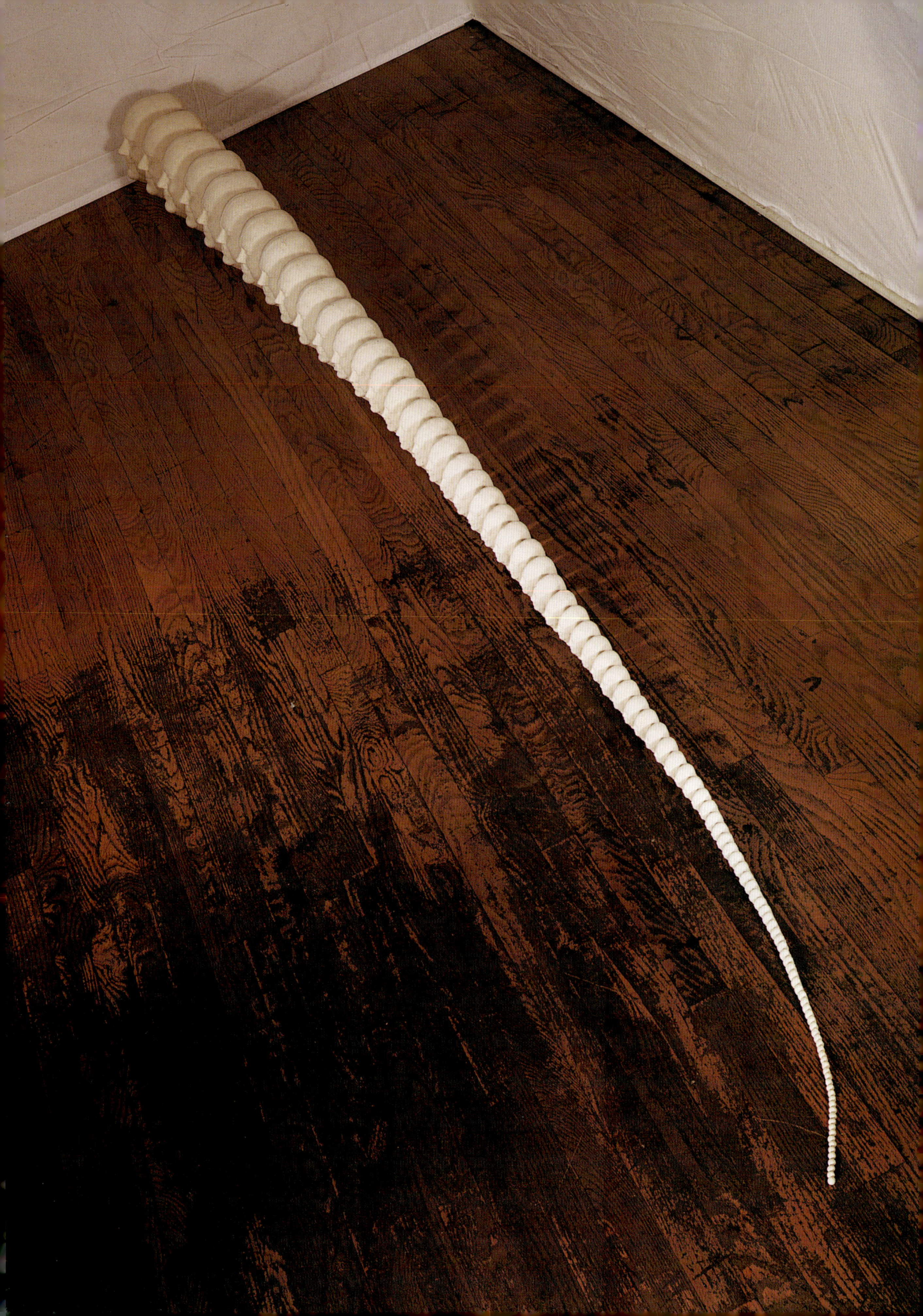

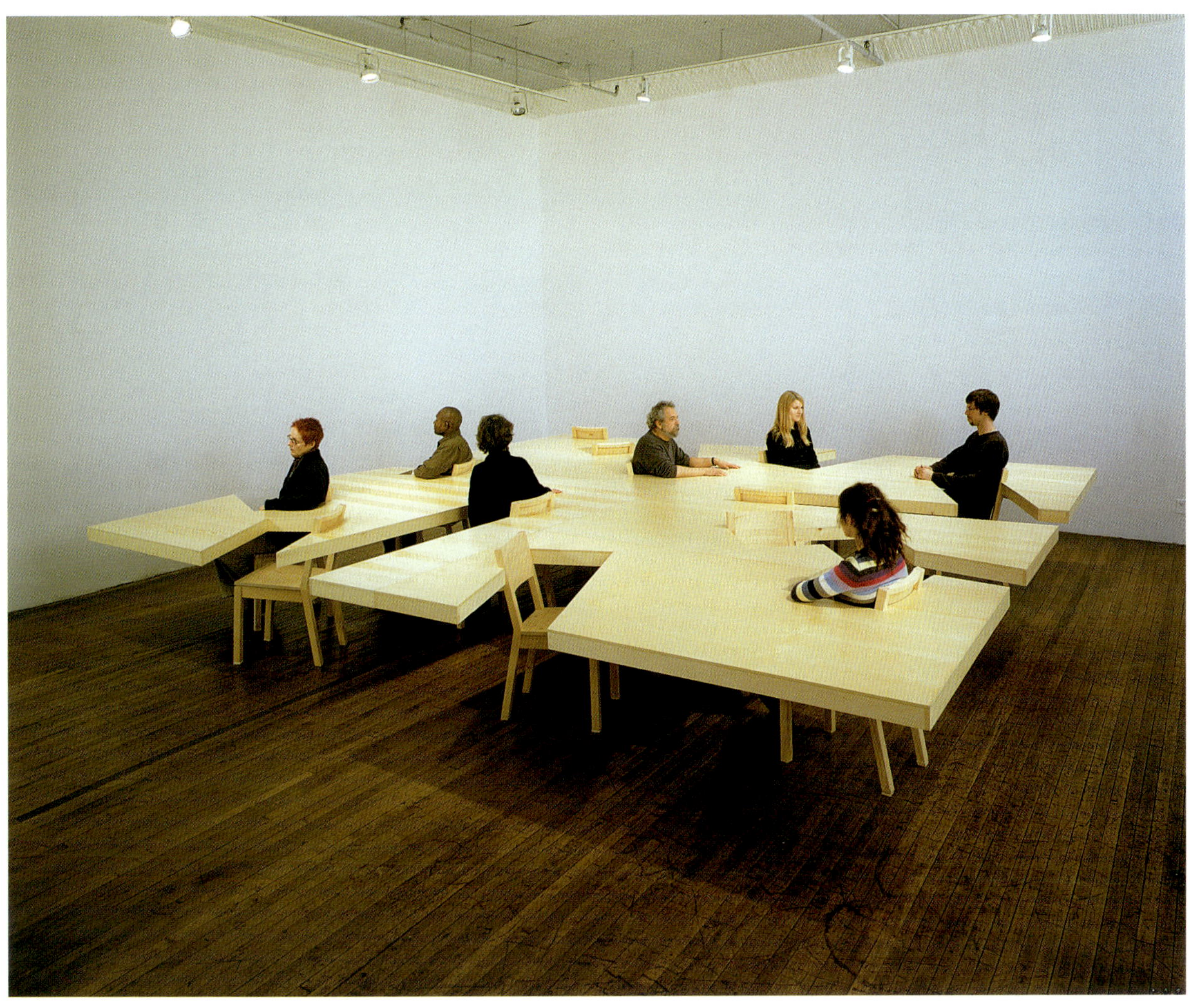

Travis Geery
Patriarchy (installation view
in the artist's studio), 2002

Ceramic
Dimensions variable
Courtesy of the artist

Alan Wexler
Too Large Table (installation view at
Ronald Feldman Fine Art, New York), 2002

Pine
30 x 192 x 192
Courtesy Ronald Feldman Fine Art, New York

Mark Bennett
Home of: George and Louise Jefferson, 2000
Ink on vellum
17 1/2 x 22 1/2 framed

Home of: Frasier Crane, 1998
Ink on graph paper
24 x 35 framed

Courtesy of the artist and the Mark Moore Gallery, Santa Monica, CA

Alan Berliner
Nobody's Business, 1996
16mm film converted to DVD, color, sound; 60 minutes
Courtesy of the artist

Sanford Biggers
Racine de Mémoire, 2002
Salvaged wood, mixed media, video projection; Super 8 film converted to DVD; sound, color
Courtesy of the artist

Richard Billingham
Untitled, 1991
Black and white print mounted on aluminum
38 1/2 x 58

Untitled, 1991
Black and white print mounted on aluminum
67 x 46

Courtesy Anthony Reynolds Gallery, London

Louise Bourgeois
Couple, 2001
Fabric
20 x 6 1/4

Courtesy of the artist and Cheim & Read, New York

Geneviève Cadieux
Elle et Lui, 1997
Diptych; chromogenic print mounted on Plexiglas with aluminum frame
77 1/2 x 62 1/2
The Bailey Collection, Toronto, Ontario

Sophie Calle
Autobiographies (The Rival), 1992
Silver gelatin print, text panel
86 x 38 1/4

Autobiographies (Amnesia), 1992
Silver gelatin print, text panel
86 x 38 1/4

Courtesy of the artist and Paula Cooper Gallery, New York

Chrissy Conant
Chrissy Caviar, 2001-02
Human eggs, human tubal fluid, liquid silicone, polyethyline, nylon, glass, brass, refrigeration equipment
52 x 49 x 47

Chrissy Caviar, 2001-02
Giclée print, #1/100
33 x 23 1/2

Courtesy of the artist

John Corbin
1000 Plateaus: Alliances and Liaisons, 1998/2002
Acrylic globes, copper tubing, polymer emulsion, carpeting, light bulbs, housed in wooden construction
Dimensions variable
Courtesy of the artist

Patricia Cronin
Memorial to a Marriage, 2001-02
Cast and carved plaster
17 x 27 x 53
Courtesy of the artist

Laura Dunn
Baby, 1999
16mm film converted to DVD; black and white, sound, 5 minutes
Courtesy of the artist

Nicole Eisenman
Hunting, 2000
Oil on wood panel
43 x 56
Collection of Mr. and Mrs. Daniel M. Holtz, Miami, FL

Fishing, 2000
Oil on wood panel
43 x 56
Collection of Ivelin and Craig Robins, Miami, FL

Courtesy of the artist

Margi Geerlinks
Pinocchio, 1999
Cibachrome print, Plexiglas, dibond
50 x 67
Collection of Ikkan Sanada, New York

Travis Geery
Patriarchy, 2002
Ceramic
Dimensions variable
Courtesy of the artist

Nan Goldin
From Here to Maternity, 1986-2000/2000
24 mounted cibachrome prints
60 x 100
Courtesy Matthew Marks Gallery, New York

Doug Hall
These Are the Rules, 1983
Video; color, sound; 4:39 minutes
Courtesy of Electronic Arts Intermix, New York

Geof Huth
Words of the Family, 2002
Mixed media installation
Dimensions variable
Courtesy of the artist

Ginger Krebs
Conjoined Hanger, 1997
Steel
9 x 16 x 1 1/2
Collection of Pat Goizetti and
Therese Quinn, Chicago

Untitled, 1999
Secondhand shirts, cotton warp
63 x 48 x 2

Courtesy of the artist

Maria Marshall
*President Bill Clinton, Memphis,
Tennessee, November 13, 1993*, 2000
DVD projection; color, sound,
1:23 minute loop
Courtesy of the artist and Team
Gallery, New York

Josiah McElheny
*Pledge: The First Glass Loving Cups
[Replica] Commission*, 1994
Blown glass, engraved, flame-
worked, certificate, display case
8 x 8 x 3

*Renewal: The Anniversary Passglas
[Replica] Commission*, 1994
Blown glass, engraved, flameworked, certificate, display case
15 x 4 1/2 x 4 1/2

Courtesy of the artist and Donald
Young Gallery, Chicago

Robert Melee
Me and Mommy, 2001
Slip cover, gilded frame, black and
white, and color photographs
65 1/2 x 53
Courtesy Andrew Kreps Gallery,
New York

Sean Mellyn
It's a Beautiful Day, 2000
Oil on canvas, mixed media
(29 objects)
Canvas size 96 x 60;
overall dimensions variable

Courtesy Tilton/Kustera Gallery,
New York

Olu Oguibe
Mementos, 1995
Mixed media with paper box,
dolls, fabric
5 x 20 x 22 1/2
Collection of the artist

Tatsumi Orimoto
In the Box (Mama), 1997
Photograph
23 1/2 x 27 1/2

*In the Box (Mama and
Neighbor)*, 1997
Photograph
23 1/2 x 27 1/2

*In the Box (Mama, Son and
Neighbor)*, 1997
Photograph
23 1/2 x 27 1/2

Courtesy of the artist

Adrian Piper
Ashes to Ashes, 1995
Photo-text work including:
    black and white photograph,
    48 x 30
    text panel, 48 x 24
    color photograph, 18 x 30
    color photograph, 24 x 30
Collection of the artist

Barbara Pollack
Perfect Dark, 2001
Video installation; color, sound;
4:30 minutes
Courtesy of the artist

Ernesto Pujol
*Still-life #1 (from the
Whiteness series)*, 1999
C-print photograph
8 x 13 unframed

*Still-life #3 (from the
Whiteness series)*, 1999
C-print photograph
8 x 13 unframed

Courtesy of the artist and Galeria
Ramis Barquet, New York

Christoph Raitmayr
Ikea—Storage as a Self-portrait, 2000
Wood
70 x 62 x 11
Courtesy of the artist and Galerie
Krinzinger, Vienna

Faith Ringgold
*Matisse's Chapel (The French
Collection, Part 1, #6)*, 1991
Acrylic on canvas with
fabric border
74 x 79 1/2
Collection of George and Joyce
Wein, New York
Courtesy of the artist and ACA
Galleries, New York

Mira Schor with Ilya Schor
Modest (Daughter and Father),
mid-1950s-2000
Painting installation including:
    Mira Schor, *Modest Painting*, 2000
    ink and gesso on linen; 12 x 16
    Ilya Schor, *Scribe at Home*, mid-1950s
    gouache on plywood;
    approx. 7 3/4 x 9 3/4
    Mira Schor, *Modest Painting*, 2000
    ink and gesso on linen; 12 x 16

Courtesy of Mira Schor and the
estate of Ilya Schor

Mira Schor with Resia Schor
Bold (Daughter and Mother),
1976-2002
Painting and sculpture installation
including:
　Resia Schor, *Fragmented
　Mezuzah*, 1976, brass, Plexiglas,
　gouache on paper; 12 1/4 x 6 1/2
　Mira Schor, *Inappropriate(d)ly*, 2000
　ink and gesso on linen; 12 x 16
　Resia Schor, *Fragmented
　Mezuzah,* 1976, brass, Plexiglas,
　gouache on paper; 12 x 9

Courtesy of the artists

Sandra Scolnik
Charles, 1999
Oil on wood panel
6 5/8 x 5 3/4
Collection of Frank and
Nina Moore, New York

The Sisters, 1998-99
Oil on wood panel
10 x 8 1/2
Collection of Dominique
Levy, New York

Courtesy CRG Gallery, New York

Jonathan Seliger
For A Family, 1995-96
Oil, alkyd, acrylic, modeling paste,
varnish on canvas; lacquer on steel
44 1/2 x 19 x 19
Collection of the artist

Ma & Pa (American Gothic), 2001
Oil, alkyd, acrylic, molding, paste,
varnish on canvas
112 1/2 x 3 3/4 x 3 3/4

Courtesy of the artist and Jack
Shainman Gallery, New York

Tony Tasset
I AM U R ME, 1998
Video transferred to DVD; color,
sound; 30 second loop
Courtesy Feigen Contemporary,
New York

Chris Verene
Untitled (Grandpa Bill), 1997
Chromogenic print
24 x 20

Untitled (Grandpa Bill #2), 1997
Chromogenic print
24 x 20

Untitled (Galesburg #48), 1998
Chromogenic print
24 x 20

Untitled (Galesburg #58), 1999-2000
Chromogenic print
24 x 20

Untitled (Galesburg #51), 2000
Chromogenic print
24 x 20

Courtesy of the artist and Paul
Morris Gallery, New York

Mark Wallinger
Royal Ascot, 1994
Video installation consisting of four
monitors, four DVD players, sync
unit, four speakers, four flight cases
Edition of 3
Approx. 72 x 114 x 30 3/4
Collection of the British Council
Courtesy Anthony Reynolds Gallery,
London

Allan Wexler
Too Large Table, 2002
Pine
30 x 192 x 192
Courtesy Ronald Feldman
Fine Art, New York

Jin-me Yoon
Intersection V, 2001
Framed C-prints
Diptych, 80 x 72 each
Courtesy of the artist and Catriona
Jeffries Gallery, Vancouver,
British Columbia

artists

Mark Bennett
1956 Born in Chattanooga,
Tennessee
Lives and works in Los Angeles

Alan Berliner
1956 Born in Brooklyn, New York
Lives and works in New York

Sanford Biggers
1970 Born in Los Angeles
Lives and works in New York

Richard Billingham
1970 Born in Birmingham, England
Lives and works in Stourbridge,
England

Louise Bourgeois
1911 Born in Paris
Lives and works in New York

Geneviève Cadieux
1956 Born in Montréal, Québec
Lives and works in Montréal,
Québec

Sophie Calle
1953 Born in Paris
Lives and works in Paris

Chrissy Conant
Born in Kailua, Hawaii
Lives and works in New York

John Corbin
1962 Born in Detroit, Michigan
Lives and works in Brooklyn,
New York

Pat Cronin
1963 Born in Beverly, Massachusetts
Lives and works in New York

Laura Dunn
1975 Born in New Orleans
Lives and works in Austin, Texas

Nicole Eisenman
1965 Born in Verdun, France
Lives and works in New York

Margi Geerlinks
1970 Born in Kampen,
The Netherlands
Lives and works in Rotterdam,
The Netherlands

Travis Geery
1976 Born in Lansstuhl, Germany
Lives and works in Newark,
Delaware

Nan Goldin
1953 Born in Washington D.C.
Lives and works in New York

Doug Hall
1944
Lives and works in San Francisco

Geof Huth
1960 Born in Burlingame, California
Lives in Schenectady and works in
Albany, New York

Ginger Krebs
1970 Born in Cleveland, Ohio
Lives and works in Chicago

Maria Marshall
1966 Born in Bombay, India
Lives and works in London

Josiah McElheny
1966 Born in Boston, Massachusetts
Lives and works in Brooklyn,
New York

Robert Melee
1966 Born in South Amboy,
New Jersey
Lives and works in New York

Sean Mellyn
1965 Born in Providence,
Rhode Island
Lives and works in New York

Olu Oguibe
1964 Born in Aba, Nigeria
Lives and works in New York

Tatsumi Orimoto
1946 Born in Japan
Lives and works in Kawasaki City,
Japan

Adrian Piper
1945 Born in New York
Lives and works in Hyannis,
Massachusetts

Barbara Pollack
1957 Born in Brooklyn, New York
Lives and works in New York

Ernesto Pujol
1958 Born in Cuba
Lives and works in New York

Christoph Raitmayr
1977 Born in Innsbruck, Austria
Lives and works in Vienna

Faith Ringgold
1930 Born in Harlem, New York
Lives and works in San Diego and
New Jersey

Mira Schor
1950 Born in New York
Lives and works in New York

Sandra Scolnik
1968 Born in Glens Falls, New York
Lives and works in Brooklyn,
New York

Jonathan Seliger
1955 Born in New York
Lives and works in Brooklyn,
New York

Tony Tasset
1960 Born in Cincinnati, Ohio
Lives and works in Oak Park, Illinois

Chris Verene
1969 Born in Galesburg, Illinois
Lives and works in Atlanta, Georgia

Mark Wallinger
1959 Born in Chigwell, England
Lives and works in London

Allan Wexler
1949 Born in Bridgeport,
Connecticut
Lives and works in New York

Jin-me Yoon
1960 Born in Seoul, Korea
Lives and works in Vancouver,
British Columbia

poets

Cal Bedient
1935 Born in Grand Coulee,
Washington
Lives and works in Los Angeles

W.S. Di Piero
1945 Born in South Philadelphia
Lives and works in San Francisco

Louise Glück
1943 Born in New York
Lives in Cambridge, Massachusetts

Linda Gregerson
1950 Born in Elgin, Illinois
Lives and works in Ann Arbor,
Michigan

Robert Hass
1941 Born in San Francisco
Lives in Berkeley, California

Brenda Hillman
1951 Born in Tucson, Arizona
Lives in Kensington, California

Marie Howe
Born in Rochester, New York
Lives and works in New York

Sharon Olds
1942 Born in San Francisco
Lives and works in New York

Molly Peacock
1947 Born in Buffalo, New York
Lives and works in New York and
London, Ontario

Martha Rhodes
1953 Born in Boston, Massachusetts
Lives and works in New York

curators

Jessica Hough
1971 Born in Philadelphia
Lives and works in Connecticut

Richard Klein
1955 Born in Newark, New Jersey
Lives and works in Connecticut

Claudia Matzko
1956 Born in Providence, Rhode
Island
Lives and works in Baltimore,
Maryland

Matthew McCaslin
1957 Born in Bayshore, New York
Lives and works in New York

Harry Philbrick
1958 Born in Providence, Rhode
Island
Lives and works in Connecticut

Poetry Editor
Steven Henry Madoff
1955 Born in New York
Lives and works in New York

Cal Bedient: "On Leaving My Son's Wedding Before the Cutting of the Cake" from *Candy Necklace*. Copyright © 1997 by Cal Bedient. Reprinted by permission of the poet and Wesleyan University Press, University Press of New England.

W.S. Di Piero: "White Blouse White Shirt" from *Skirts and Slacks: Poems* by W. S. Di Piero, copyright © 2001 by W. S. Di Piero. Used by permission of the poet and Alfred A. Knopf, a division of Random House, Inc.

Louise Glück: "Mother and Child" from *The Seven Ages*. Copyright © 2001 by Louise Glück. Reprinted by permission of the poet and HarperCollins Publishers Inc.

Linda Gregerson: "A History Play" from *Waterborne* by Linda Gregerson. Copyright © 2002 by Linda Gregerson. Reprinted by permission of Houghton Mifflin Company. All rights reserved

Robert Hass: "My Mother's Nipples" from *Sun Under Wood* by Robert Hass. Copyright © 1996 by Robert Hass. Reprinted by permission of the poet and HarperCollins Publishers Inc., The Ecco Press

Brenda Hillman: "Two Brothers" from *Loose Sugar*. Copyright © 1997 by Brenda Hillman. Reprinted by permission of the poet and Wesleyan University Press, University Press of New England.

Marie Howe: "Marriage" appeared in *The New Yorker*, February 18 & 25, 2002. Reprinted by permission of the poet.

Sharon Olds: "His Costume" originally appeared in *The New Yorker*. Copyright © 2000 by Sharon Olds. Reprinted by permission of the poet.

Molly Peacock: "Say You Love Me." Copyright © 1989 by Molly Peacock. Used by permission of the poet.

Martha Rhodes: "A Progression" appeared in *Fence*, Fall/Winter 2002. Reprinted by permission of the poet.

photo credits

Page 20, 21: D.W. Leitner

Page 29: Christopher Burke

Page 36, 37: Richard-Max Tremblay

Page 69: Faith Ringgold © 1991

Page 72: Electronic Arts Intermix

Page 78: Olu Oguibe

Page 80, 81: Chris Gergley

Page 86: David Appel

Page 87: Dennis Cowley